Little Ethan Lopez has touched
a community together. People ha
been saved, friends have come together, and a community has been
strengthened. He has made more of an impact on this earth in his
short life than many will make in a lifetime.

Kendall B.

As thousands prayed and are grieving, many are rejoicing in the
miracles that God did perform. Though we may not see the good in
the pain that is felt, the good that we see of lives saved by Ethan is
reassuring. One baby boy changed the lives of so many and has
personally changed my life and my walk with God.

Elizabeth J.

As we celebrated Ethan's life today, I gained a whole new perspective
on what it means to rely on God's strength. Some wonder in times
like these, where is God? I saw Him today. Ethan's parents, Sam and
Kristen, displayed amazing peace today that only He can provide.

Gina W.

Wow! Kristen, you are such an inspiration. This blog brought me to
tears. Through your pain and suffering you are teaching me and others
how important it is to let go and let God. I want to have the faith you
and Sam have shown. It definitely has been eye opening!

Rhianna R.

Kristen, thank you so much for continuing to share your story. Your
honesty and raw emotion has been an inspiration to not only myself
but many others. To see how God is working in your life, is amazing!

Christina W.

Miracles are not always what we think they should be. Our perspective
is so limited. But God sees all. And He is good.

Kristen J.

Kristen and Sam, we wanted to be of some encouragement to you today, but the grace, strength, peace, and passion that you carried yourself with left us all more encouraged, challenged, and changed at the end. Thank you for sharing your little rock star with us. Heaven's worship band just got better and brighter. I look forward to hearing him play and am confident the crowd in heaven will be a little larger because of how he lived and because of your bold witness.

John C.

Many would question and blame God for this tragic loss not understanding why He would allow such an innocent life to be taken. You both have displayed such a trust in Him over the last few days that even though the reasons may not be apparent, some of the effects are! Through your courage and strength, little Ethan has had a great impact on thousands of lives and will continue to do so. We may never know all of the reasons why this happened, but you will always be part of the positive effect in changing people's lives.

Greg T.

I can truly say that another family's trial, suffering, and heartbreak as well as faith, strength, hope, and peace has and is forever changing my life. Ethan's story daily continues to move and inspire me. Only God can do great things in the midst of such tragedy and bring peace when there seems to be none.

Marcy L.

I am coming to realize that HOPE is the difference between faith and religion. Hope drives us to ask big, expect big, love big, and fearlessly. Hope is also the very hardest part of faith in this incredibly broken world. Today people all over the country and all over the world are laying their souls bare with HOPE expecting big, asking big and loving BIG for a little boy named Ethan.

Alicia D.

Lessons from a
Rock Star

Rocked to the core while encountering God's

supernatural peace, joy, hope and love.

Kristen Lopez

ISBN 978-0692888629

Editing by Kristen Jacobs

Cover design by Panagiotis Lampridis

Photography by Luminosity Photography and Design
(excluding About the Author page)

Printed and bound in USA.
First Printing May 2017

1 2 3 4 5 6 7 8 9 10

To Sam

"When nothing makes sense and every thought is blurred, love finds a way." Your words, God's promise since the beginnings of the existence of 'us.'

The only reason I am standing today is because God thought it perfect for me to stand beside you... always.

[contents]

INTRODUCTION

PART 1 – BLOG

PART 2 – THIS IS NOT THE END

[intro]

TODAY WAS A GOOD DAY

Makeup and hair gadgets spread across the dining room table. The bustle of our family stirred throughout our packed-out house, their luggage and clothes seemingly scattered in every corner from their arrival the days and nights prior. There was a constant buzz of chatter, planning and strategizing the events of the day. Every now and then, my husband, Sam, would not so gently remind everyone by yelling loudly, "T minus 60!" and so on, as the time we needed to whisk ourselves out the door dwindled down. Showers ran constantly, people running up and down the stairs. Phones sounded and the doorbell rang numerous times throughout the morning for breakfast deliveries from work friends, dry cleaner deliveries, and additional family that eventually showed up. Needless to say, our barking dog, Bono, was not a happy camper with all this chaos spinning around him early that morning on May 23, 2012.

The loud whirring of a blow dryer in my ear was almost soothing, helping to momentarily drown out the feelings of butterflies that were insistent on fluttering in the pit of my stomach.

Is this really my life right now? Is this all about to go down?

As Sam's cousin forcefully tugged at a layer of my hair with her hairstyling tools and blower, I sat there at the dining room table in the midst of it all as I carefully gave my best attempt to apply some soft, rosy blush to my niece's cheeks.

The emotion was peculiar. Conflicted. I felt queasy. And the lump in my throat swelled more prominently than I had ever experienced in my life.

But I don't think anyone that went through these moments in our house that morning could shake a sense, not just an unnerving anticipation, but of something unexpected. The activity comforted me, not just because I was surrounded by people I loved and who loved me, but all of it communicated to me an excitement, an awareness that something momentous and special was about to happen. And this impression I believe, was perceived by all.

For lack of a better comparison, it oddly resembled all the commotion that goes into the morning of a wedding (minus the bride and dresses, of course.) In fact, in the very moments of awakening that morning, I was struck by a déjà vu of sorts. I was hit by the same anticipation that accompanies attending a significant event, one that Sam and I planned that would change the course of our lives. I felt the same uneasiness of entering into an inescapable day. And in both instances, I felt the same pressures of being thrown into the center of attention. But most of all, I woke up in an expectancy to walk through a day of hope. A hope to celebrate something so special, a celebration of a great powerful love and the hope of life.

Only the night before, our house was seeping of song and praise. I adamantly warned Sam the afternoon before that we must attain some quality rest. I rigidly insisted we get to bed early so that we could wake up fresh for a day that would most likely drain the life out of us. Well, who was I kidding, forgetting the craziness and festivity we always fall into when Sam's cousins and siblings unite, yes, even during a time like this? We ended up staying up until three in the morning laughing and playing with Sam's family (rock stars in their own right) singing and practicing songs we would sing the next day, windows wide open for the neighborhood to hear.

Does it even make sense? Is there a right and wrong way to go about this? Is it even possible to begin to conceptualize this day ahead of us, to even begin to imagine or even put into words or song?

There was a lot of planning that went into it, heaps of passion, gallons of tears shed, and boundless love...

But how can you begin to imagine the day you are forced to bury your son?

I grabbed a muffin in the whirlwind. I knew I would have to shove it down my throat for the sole purposes of getting some sustenance in my body before rushing out the door into hours of events that were about to unfold. I collapsed on the couch in the living room as I gulped down an oversized, dry bite.

I couldn't escape my son, Ethan's, newborn pictures staring at me on the wooden shelf on the opposite wall. He was only six days old when he started his little "modeling career" in front of the camera, although, in this shoot all he did was sleep. In one picture he lay in a wooden basket wearing nothing but his tiny newborn diaper, his pudgy belly and legs scrunched together in the fetal position as if he was still living inside me. In the other picture, one of my favorites, he is swaddled in a white blanket laying on his back on a white, fuzzy rug sporting his black hat that says, "Rock." What can I say? The kid was born a rock star.

Memories came in like a flood. The first week of Ethan's life welcomed me with terrible disorientation. Did I even manage more than three hours of sleep over the course of the whole week?

I remember so clearly the engulfing exhaustion as I awoke for the photoshoot that morning. The amount of paraphernalia, bags, and gadgets I had to remember to lug along with me on my first ever excursion with Ethan, felt absurd. Talk about a hot mess. I'd be surprised if I actually looked in the mirror that morning or even cared if I stepped into the shower. I was terrified and rudely awakened by the idea that this was now the new reality of the path my life was taking. I could no longer ease on out in style, matching sunglasses to my outfit, keys in hand and purse on my shoulder as I swiftly graced myself out the door. No. Leaving the house was now this big clumsy production that I was afraid I would never master.

As I sat there in the flashback, I came to find all of those fears so silly. I would do anything to go back to that place, no matter how sleep deprived or delirious I felt. How could I ever expect that morning as I awkwardly lugged his car seat out the door for the first time, fumbling with keys, desperately attempting not to fall down our concrete steps, that only twenty months later I would sit on the couch face to face with the very pictures that were to be taken that day? That those very pictures would serve as some of the only tangible memories I had to cling to of my precious son, Ethan, etched on my heart for as long as I live in this life.

Ethan looked so peaceful, so content, so free from the cares of this world. How I longed to experience even a fraction of that state of sheer euphoria and calm. Was I jealous of Ethan, knowing that what he really was experiencing was probably an exaggerated version of what those pictures portrayed? How I yearned to be where he was. How I hungered for this pit of fear to remove its grip from my now grief-stricken life.

Desperate for a hope-jolt, I pulled out my phone and opened my Bible app. In those moments I didn't realize the depth of the power that was to follow my reading a simple verse in the book of Thessalonians. Those words set the tone for the minutes, hours, days, months, and years to come as I embarked on this new journey of grief. More than a mere jolt, the words jumped out of my phone and penetrated the message of hope into the dark cavernous depths of my being.

> And now dear brothers and sisters, we want you to know what will happen to believers who have died so you will not grieve like people who have no hope. (Thess. 4:13)

So you will not grieve like people who have no hope.

That hope, a hope that will be unveiled throughout these pages. A hope and faith I believed and committed my life to for years prior, suddenly just got real. Like… smacked-me-in-the-face kind of real. This was a true test of what hope was left in my life.

Hope.

You may not ever have to endure the loss of a child, God forbid. And if you have, my heart bears witness to your agonizing pain. As long as you are a living, breathing, and feeling human, however, you will no doubt go through a season (or two or a hundred and two) in life that brings a loss in one form or another. A loss of a loved one, loss of a friend, loss of dignity, loss of physical mobility, loss of a job, loss of a good reputation, loss of control, loss of possessions, loss of trust, loss of acceptance, loss of freedom, loss of a dream, loss of the will to live, or any loss in your life that rocks you to your core.

Maybe you've already experienced the crushing wreckage of a storm in your life. Maybe you are currently in the midst of the damaging gale-force winds. Or worse, your entire life has been one long downpour that refuses to let up in accumulation of loss after loss after loss. And contrary, if you have avoided these storms thus far, unfortunately, the odds are against you that you will find yourself drenched in a storm in your near future.

Can you imagine how drastically different that season would look if through that trial, you gained a new perspective, saw through a new set of lenses, and had access to this hope that brings peace, joy, and love?

I clung to the hope I knew that day and every single day of my life thereafter. God gave me new lenses to see life through.

I felt God's presence and strength that allowed me to get up from that couch and take the next few steps I needed to take to get out of the door and face this unfathomable yet ironically bittersweet and beautiful day. Never in a million years would I have ever expected at the end of a day full of death, celebration, loss, worship, tears, life, burial, pain and, yes, laughter and joy, the words that proceeded forth from my mouth.

At the end of the day we buried our son, I admitted to Sam:

"Today was a good day." And he agreed.

Looking back, it is incomprehensible. The enigmatic peace I experienced was baffling.

That doesn't take away from the gut-wrenching, heart-shattering-into-a-gazillion-miniscule-pieces kind of pulverizing pain I contested with in the days and weeks following his death. So, it's not that my experience of peace in the pain comes from living in denial or detachment from reality. My husband and I went through extensive counseling, sometimes being exposed to therapy as much as three to four times a week between the both of us.

That said, I consider myself to be one of the weakest, most broken, most fearfully paralyzed people on the planet outside of the grace of God. I had already been down the hellish road of over ten long years of varying seasons of numbing depression, debilitating anxiety, and a mental condition or two associated with both, before Ethan's crisis began. Clearly I am the weakest of the weak. However, I cannot deny God's indisputable presence in the course of events that unfolded surrounding Ethan's death and in the grief process that unraveled thereafter.

Quite possibly over the course of your reading this book, you may find yourself asking the question, "Okay now, is she for real?" My prayer is that you can welcome the authenticity of my testimony and realize that it is hard for even my own self to wrap my head around it all. I believe it can only be explained by the mystery of God's unfathomable love for mankind.

Because I have responded to great hardship on such opposing ends of the spectrum at different points in my life, from intense bitterness on one end to trusting acceptance and peace on the extreme opposite, I believe I have the ability to offer reflective wisdom. I humbly propose my reflection has lifechanging potential for you. I share more in depth about these two opposing responses to hardship and the impacts thereof in Part Two, "This is Not the End."

Just a week after Ethan left this life to spend an eternity with Jesus, and five years from the time of writing this book, I was inspired to start a blog I called "Lessons From a Rock Star." I was oblivious at the time where the blog would lead me or how deeply it would reach the people around me. All I knew was that the well of words and stories and memories needed to gush out of my heart and soul through my keyboard-pounding fingertips. It didn't take long for me to realize that the lessons I had learned from Ethan weren't just meant for me to selflessly bottle up. But were meant to bless others and flood the world.

In this book I share with you each post of my blog spanning a three-month period of time directly following the passing of Ethan. Over the course of those three months, I encountered and lived in the peace that goes beyond all understanding, with a joy unspeakable, a hope secure in Jesus, and an everlasting love.

I strongly and lovingly encourage you to take the time to really allow yourself to go on your own journey as you read through the chapters and blog entries in this book. In Part One, challenge yourself to go deeper with a heart of openness and humility to answer the questions at the end of each chapter.

Part Two holds what I believe to be the most life transforming and profound message as I reflect back through these five years of my journey spent missing Ethan. Therein lies the greatest lessons. Lessons that can easily be taken for granted and momentarily forgotten unless I remind myself through prayer. I have included prayers that I use to keep these principles at the forefront of my thoughts. If you desire a greater awareness of these spiritual guidelines for your life, use these prayers as a model for your personal times of reflection. After the prayers, I've highlighted verses that have spoken promise over me through the transforming power of their truths.

My hope is that by your reading through to the end, you would reach new heights encountering a supernatural peace, joy, hope, and love on levels you may have never experienced before.

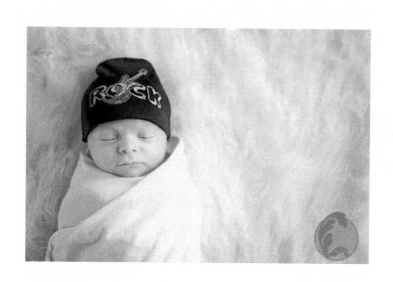

PART ONE

LESSONS FROM A ROCK STAR BLOG

HE ROCKED OUR LIVES.

HE ROCKED OUR HEARTS.

WE WILL NEVER BE THE SAME.

#LESSONSFROMAROCKSTAR

[one]

ROCKED TO THE CORE

May 29, 2012

I figured I'd take the giant, scary leap into the world of blogging. Even before my world turned upside-down only two weeks ago, I felt drawn towards this outlet of sharing a piece of me with the online world. Up until now, however, I didn't really have anything (meaningful or interesting enough) to say.

My world finally felt perfect. The child that Sam, my husband of nine years, and I had prayed for for many years just turned twenty months old. My life was filled with Mickey and puzzles and crayons and soccer balls and drumsticks and birdies and playgrounds and stickers and sunny days and drumsticks and bubbles and monkeys and choo-choo trains (did I mention drumsticks?) and LIFE, lived to the fullest through my son, Ethan Isaac. I realized a few months ago that being a mother was what I was born to be and nothing else in this world could fill my heart with such purpose and pleasure.

Ethan was my world. Ethan was Sam's world. We revolved our whole lives around him, from my deciding to work part-time to Sam's decision and strong desire to do the same. The way God had given us the opportunity to do so was the perfect scenario. We planned our vacations around him, weekends around him, and took him everywhere we went. We wanted him to experience life. And in doing so, we experienced life through him.

Just two weeks ago our dreams shattered, hearts rocked to the core. Our little rock star, Ethan, went into cardiac arrest from a fever leading to an uncontrollable seizure. After forty minutes of doctors trying to revive him, no words can describe the feeling of being sat down and told that your otherwise healthy and happy son...

...died.

I can only describe it as numbing feelings of a surreal haze of being, yet not present in reality. I had never been so detached from reality in my life.

Being more present in the moment than I, his daddy's love went so deep that he literally pushed over a nurse to get to his child and beg him to come back to life.

"You're a scrapper, buddy! Come back! Daddy says so!" Almost immediately... *beep, beep, beep*... heartbeat... relief and joy... at least in that moment...

Ethan Isaac passed on to his heavenly Daddy after being in a coma for four days.

Now. This is the start of my new life. I have chosen to accept this life-shaking detour in the road by the strength of God and faith knowing that His ways are greater and higher. I don't know where I'm headed. The road ahead is scary. The journey will be long. I don't have all the answers.

What I do know is that this little rock star rocked our lives. He rocked our hearts. We will never be the same

Go Deeper:

1. What has been the greatest life-shaking detour you have ever taken?

2. What scared you the most about facing the unknown of that situation?

3. Did that detour rock you to your core? If so, in what ways have you changed? In what ways have you stayed the same?

[two]

DIAPER CHANGES SUCK

June 1, 2012

I am a very private person. That said, it is ironic that I have to start out with a disclaimer saying that there is a bit of 'crazy' in this post. It is nerve-wracking bearing my soul, but at the same time I've found it to be freeing and cathartic, so I succumb.

One of the biggest and clearest lessons I learned from Ethan was during one of his routine diaper changes when he was around six months old. He lay there on our bed as I persistently yet unsuccessfully tried to pin him down as his arms and legs flailed desperately. He cried and fussed in anger as if I had the nerve to disrupt his life for a mere five seconds to take care of his needs.

I remember gently but firmly telling him, "Ethan, I know this process isn't fun, but the quicker you remain still and let go and trust me, the quicker and easier we will both get through this." Immediately in that moment God turned this statement right around on me and replaced his name with my name. I stood there as I was trying to snap his onesie back together watching Ethan flail. In that moment, I saw myself.

The whole first spring and summer of Ethan's life was one of the many times in my life that I suffered with severe anxiety. (Looking back, I am certain this flare up was due to postpartum depression.) Because I had such a long and frustrating battle with anxiety in the past, I was devastated to find out that it had crept its ugly head back in my life at the most inconvenient time, at a time when I wanted to live out the summer to the fullest with Ethan. Go to the beach, go on picnics and adventures, walks, travel and explore the world. So...

Here it goes... I promised you some crazy...

One of my anxieties prevented me from being in the sun and eventually, at my lowest and most debilitating days, being exposed to light. I was trapped in a world of darkness and depression, non-functional as a mother and downright angry and bitter towards God. *How could God allow this in my life, yet again?! Why couldn't He just heal me miraculously then and there!?*

I kicked and screamed. I squirmed and pounded my fists at God for a good two months, at least.

"Kristen, I know this process isn't fun, but the quicker you remain still and let go and trust me, the quicker we will both get through this."

Hearing these words stunned me and hit me deep and hard. It took a few days to digest, but I finally realized I needed to stop crying like a baby. I, myself, chose to waste all that time kicking and screaming. Going through the "diaper change" sucked, but the quicker I remained still and gave up my reigns to Him, the quicker God brought me to freedom.

The day I surrendered to the *process*, God immediately started working.

Wouldn't it be stupid to make this same mistake I had been making in my life over and over again? As I am utterly crushed and broken from Ethan's passing, I almost had no choice other than to completely surrender to God's process. I know the result if I don't... frustration, anger, bitterness, and misery will be right around the corner. Instead, I want the freedom, hope, comfort, and blessing of God that He promises. Because of this surrendered choice, I learned that surrendering to the process isn't just about giving up control. It's about discovering freedom.

My circumstances suck. That's a big fat, YES! But surrendering and allowing God to work in me and through me has set me free. He has wrapped His loving arms around me and has given me a peace that goes beyond all understanding, the comfort He promises in mourning, and a closeness to Him that I've never experienced before.

Go Deeper:

1. What situation in your life has caused you to kick and scream in frustration towards God?

2. What were your fears that kept you from surrendering to the process in that situation?

3. What steps can you take to still your soul and surrender?

SURRENDERING TO THE PROCESS
ISN'T JUST ABOUT GIVING UP
CONTROL. IT'S ABOUT DISCOVERING
FREEDOM.

#LESSONSFROMAROCKSTAR

[three]

JESUS HAS A BOO-BOO

June 4, 2012

The first time I introduced Ethan to Jesus was during bath time. Right around the time of his first birthday, I took away his baby bath toys consisting of cups, boats and duckies and replaced them with big boy bath toys—colorful rubber letters and numbers and some water-resistant bath books. I had so much fun every night as I taught him his colors, letters, and numbers, and I believe he had more of a blast learning them. Ethan just soaked it all in like a sponge, literally and figuratively, just like he did everything else in his life.

By the time he was sixteen months old, he knew all of his colors, and by eighteen months, all of his numbers and most letters along with the sound and a word corresponding to each letter. I would quiz him, he would quiz me, he would "spell" out "words," and at the end of bath time, pull up the drain only *after* organizing all of them on the ledge of the tub *by color*. We had quite the bath time routine going on.

'J' happened to be one of the latter letters I introduced to him. I chose no other word for the letter 'J' than Jesus, as it was the first and most obvious word that popped into my head at the time. Even though at first he didn't know what a "Jesus" was, he picked up pretty quickly and would say "J for Jesus" whenever I showed him his purple letter 'J.'

Shortly after introducing "J for Jesus," I decided that I should probably clue him in on Jesus. One night after his bath, EVOO rub-down (Daddy always thought he smelled like a salad afterwards), change into PJ's, a tooth brush, and a hair comb, we sat together in the glider for milk time.

I decided to tell him about Jesus, but not knowing how to introduce a 1-year-old to a person you can't practically see, touch, or hear, all I could come up with was, "Ethan, Jesus loves you. Jesus loves Mommy and Daddy, too. Jesus loves Ethan so much that His love for Ethan is so far greater than Mommy and Daddy could ever love him."

Not knowing if he grasped the concept of Jesus, I would repeat this to him every night during our prayers on the glider. He would put his two tiny hands together along with Mommy, and together we prayed for everyone in his little world including family, his baby cousins, and his best friend, Eli. Of course, we couldn't forget all of the doggies in his life, too—Bono, Susie, and Mimi. He would always repeat, "Men," at the end and he would then be happy to snuggle up in his crib and drift off into dreamland.

One night a couple months ago, when I was telling Ethan how much Jesus loves him, he told me as he pointed to his crib, "Jesus boo-boo. Jesus sleeping."

I giggled and said, "You're silly, Jesus doesn't have a..." But in the middle of my response, I caught myself, stunned. *Um, hello! Yes... yes! Jesus does have a boo-boo!* I corrected myself in disbelief and told him that, in fact, he was right, that Jesus had boo-boos on his hands and feet out of His love for us.

From then on, whenever I would mention Jesus, Ethan would point to his crib and say, "Jesus sleeping." At that point, the thought quickly crossed my mind of the mere chance that he had some kind of encounter with Jesus. Although staggering, it was hard for me to take this thought seriously, and I didn't even mention it to Sam at the time.

I, myself, am convinced now more than ever that out of God's love and foreknowledge, He prepared Ethan's heart. God prepared him for that moment when Jesus would invite him into a life spent in eternity with Him when his earthly body would no longer sustain him. I believe with all my heart that Ethan knew Jesus personally before he passed, whether it was through a dream in his sleep, or in whatever way that God chose to work. Ethan knew Jesus while he was still living on this earth.

I believe Ethan, now in heaven, understands *why* Jesus has a boo-boo, probably better than any of us can comprehend here. Those "boo boos" Jesus bears and will bear for all eternity are a reminder of God the Father's love for all those who have ever lived and whoever will live on this earth.

It was twelve years ago that I learned that I am not going to heaven because I'm a "good person," or because I haven't murdered anyone lately, or because I give towards the Red Cross, or because I go to church every Sunday. Because, let's face it, there's absolutely nothing spectacular enough I could ever do that would ever merit me the right to live in a perfect heaven with a perfect God.

God sent His only Son, Jesus Christ to this world... to die. The only One *blameless*, took *on* the blame of the entire world through the shedding of his blood and sacrifice on the cross... and paid the penalty for our sin.

God loved us so much that He sent His only Son... to *die*... for *you*... so that *you* can *live*.

Those who choose to believe and open their heart to a relationship with Him by faith through His grace can one day spend eternity with God.

Now that my only son, Ethan Isaac, has passed, I believe Sam and I have been given a taste of the utterly heart-wrenching sacrificial pain that the Father and Jesus's mother sorely endured. The ultimate Sacrifice was made... out of pure unconditional Love, so that hearts would be forever changed and lives saved into all eternity.

Go Deeper:

1. What does the term "unconditional love" mean to you?

2. Who in this world has come the closest to demonstrating this kind of love towards you? In what ways do you demonstrate your unconditional love for someone else?

3. What does the sacrifice of Jesus mean to you?

[four]

LIGHT ON, LIGHT OFF

June 7, 2012

If drumsticks were Ethan's one obsession, lights were his other. He was fascinated with any kind of—lightbulbs, street lights, stop lights, candlelight, moonlight, the tiny lights that show an electronic device is on, flashlights, phone lights and even the light that gets turned on in the intro of Mickey Mouse Clubhouse, which was his favorite part of the show.

Light, or "ight," also happened to be Ethan's first word besides "dada," spoken well before he ever managed to say "mama," months later. (No, I'm not bitter.)

He absolutely couldn't get enough of lights.

You could also imagine the danger involved with this obsession. Now, he wasn't just fascinated with lights themselves. He was obsessed, and I mean obsessed, with turning light switches on and off. The grandparents would be the ones to get suckered into holding him in their arms for twenty minutes as he flicked the switch up and said, "ight on," and then down, "ight off," and repeated it 500 more times. If it was up to him, he could probably play the same monotonous game for an hour or more. When Grammy or Gramps would set him down, he would pull at their heartstrings and cry for more "ight on, ight off" and of course they couldn't help but not give him what he wanted... every time.

It's no wonder how God has used this child who was so infatuated with the concept of light, as one to be set out and set apart, shining brightly as a light for the world to see. It's almost as if God chose to put this enormous spotlight on him and his short life of almost two years to make all eyes, during the unfortunate events that ensued, converge and focus on Ethan.

Because of Ethan's rock star life, rock star cuteness, and rock star image that suddenly and unexpectedly spiraled into tragedy, God grabbed people's attention through Ethan in a way that as they turned their eyes on Ethan, they ultimately were turning their eyes towards God.

I feel like during these circumstances, I've experienced enormous amounts of God's light, and I believe a huge part of that has to do with all the prayers that have gone, and continue to go, up to heaven for our family that we are so grateful for. Although I feel at peace overall, it is crazy how in one moment I can feel encouraged and filled, and in the next moment my whole world caves in and crumbles.

I can't help but see it as a light switch. When I'm focused on God's bigger picture and purpose, the lights are on, but as soon as I take my eyes off of Him and allow myself to drift into desperation, that is where everything goes pitch black. That said, I do understand there has to be tears, anguish, sadness, and mourning through the process to grow and heal, but I feel like there is a difference between mourning... and utter doom.

Where there is light there is hope.

God's light is where hearts are touched and forever changed. It is in the manifestation of the light that God speaks. It is up to us to listen. It is up to us to believe. It is up to us to act. It is up to us to love. It is up to us to *be* the light He has called us to be so that others can see the light of God in us... so that *their* hearts may be forever changed.

Could you imagine the resulting power if we all allowed our light to shine as brightly as Ethan has? God is calling us to shine His light within us so radiantly, that in unity, we can transform and illuminate the world.

You are the light of the world. A town built on a hill cannot be hidden. Neither do people light a lamp and put it under a bowl. Instead they put it on its stand, and it gives light to everyone in the house. In the same way, let your light shine before others, that they may see your good deeds and glorify your Father in heaven. (Matthew 5:14-16)

I can only begin to imagine the look, his demeanor, the marvel and awe on Ethan's face as he gazed up towards heaven and witnessed the One True Light for the first time. I can only guess as to the words he spoke as he pointed passionately, "Ight on!" or if he stood speechless because he was so captivated by God's brilliance.

As a silly side-note, I'm also curious as to Ethan's reaction when he found out that there are no light switches in heaven to turn the light off. I'd have to say he just may have been a little bit disappointed at first. I would imagine, however, that's something he got over pretty quickly.

Go Deeper:

1. Is there a family member, friend, neighbor, etc., who comes to mind when you think of someone who constantly emits "light" (positive life and hope) when you are around them? What are the characteristics about them that make them so captivating?

2. When has the "light" in other people's lives helped you through a time when all you saw was darkness?

3. When have you emitted "light" to others? What are the characteristics of that light in you? What ways can that light dispel others' darkness?

WHERE THERE IS LIGHT THERE IS HOPE.

#LESSONSFROMAROCKSTAR

[five]

NO MORE PACIFIERS

June 10, 2012

What a difficult time it's been learning to deal with this new life lived without my little boy. I had become so comfortable and happy living my every day for Ethan. The adjustment to the newborn stage and all the responsibilities that bombarded my life when Ethan was born came with quite the shock. But how much more intensely overwhelming has it been to have these responsibilities and complications of life become abruptly nonexistent?

For instance, there have been moments recently where I happen to be around a child who is acting fussy. I automatically have this innate compulsion to dig deep down in my purse to pull out what once were necessary life savers to carry around with me while out in public with Ethan—pacifiers when he was younger (at one point in time we had a total of eight or more)—toys, cars, books, crayons, cookies—basically any tool that could be used to divert an immanent meltdown.

It is with a sinking heart that I remind myself that I no longer have the need to carry these once dire necessities in my purse, and I am thrown for a loop.

No more pacifiers... a reminder that he is not here.

There are other instances where I, for a moment, refrain from yelling downstairs to call Sam from our bedroom when it is late at night, thinking there is a baby sleeping that we need not wake. The realization of the fact that I can be as loud as I need to be is a reminder that he is not here.

I no longer need to wake up (although I still do) to welcome Ethan into our bed after Daddy can't resist the urge to jump out of bed, literally running to his room every morning immediately after he hears Ethan yell, "Daddy, up... daddy, up!"

When I still wake at 6am without hearing Ethan's urgent request, again, it is a reminder he is not here.

I no longer need to make sure I have fresh milk in a sippy cup to provide at any given moment or a good supply of bananas or plain yogurt (his favorite) at home. Sometimes I have to remind myself I no longer need to block out the chunk of time between 1 and 4pm for a nap or make sure nothing gets scheduled during that time lest I end up with an angry baby later on. I no longer need to pack three bags while going out to any given place or event. I no longer have to worry about keeping the cabinets locked and the gate shut or worry about being downstairs at night without the monitor in the room... All are reminders that he is not here.

This is a very hard pill to swallow. He is not here.

I am then reminded that Ethan has left something behind for us. Until that extraordinary moment I get to be reunited with him again for all eternity, he has left us with memories cherished and a legacy that will live on.

In addition though, he has left something very special for a very chosen few. We were notified of the official news this past week from Donate Life in a letter stating that Ethan saved an infant girl's life who either had a life threatening liver disease or liver failure (specifics were not provided), as he had given his liver. In addition, a fifty-year-old woman's quality of life has been improved dramatically now that she is no longer forced and bound to the debilitating restraints of dialysis, as he has given her his two kidneys. There is a great chance that his heart valves will be used to save a number of children in the future. What an incredible blessing he has been for these individuals and their families, as part of him is present with us living on in a chosen few here on earth.

Just as Ethan has left a part of himself behind, God chose to leave a part of Himself behind for us. The story didn't end when Jesus Christ left this world as He was put to death and resurrected to heaven. He did not leave us alone on this earth to fend off evil and suffering and sickness and disease and injustice on our own.

God left behind His Spirit... His Spirit is awakened in our hearts for those who choose to *believe and invite him.*

God can live in us.

Okay, let me say it again... God... yes... the Creator of the universe, for those who choose to invite him... can live *in* us.

35

We are not alone. He is with us. He is guiding us. He is our pacifier. He is our strength. He helps us to love. His heart becomes our own when we choose to hear His Spirit.

God's purpose for us is not just to allow our eternal destinies to be altered from darkness to light. His purpose is also to help sustain us in this life so that we would express the heart of God to others... so that others would see God in us and want the same for themselves.

My life is far from perfect even though the Spirit of God lives in my heart, but His comfort amidst my suffering never fails. His direction in the crossroads of life is not absent. His wisdom amidst my confusion shines through. His love stretches way beyond my imperfections.

Ethan has left part of himself behind in order to improve and sustain people's lives here on earth just as God has left His Spirit, a pacifier to sustain us. What a comfort it is to know that we are not alone.

He is present. He is here.

Go Deeper:

1. What daily "pacifier" can you not go without (i.e. coffee, exercise, quiet time in the morning)? How does this pacifier help to comfort you?

2. What sort of spiritual practices bring you comfort and assurance when life gets a bit crazy? How?

3. Do you sense the presence of God in your life and speaking to your heart? If yes, under what circumstances do you sense His presence and voice the most? If no, what are the barriers you believe are getting in the way?

[six]

HOLD ON TIGHT

June 14, 2012

I t was only two days before the event that sent Ethan to the hospital of no return. That Monday we spent together some of the last memorable moments that I will cherish in my heart forever.

I'll never forget as I anxiously awaited Sam and Ethan's arrival as I stood in the playground area downstairs at our gym. We had just joined this gym weeks earlier and were so excited about everything it had to offer for our whole family. Some of what our membership included for Ethan were two hours of free child care a day, use of the over-the-top indoor and outdoor children-friendly pools and water slides, a whole indoor-playground area designated for kids to run around and climb, and when Ethan got older, free gymnastics, dance, or karate classes. I call it the gym on steroids (for lack of a better word.)

It was my absolute delight to watch Ethan play and laugh on the playground and splash around in the pool as Sam, Ethan, and I just started our new, almost daily routine spent at this place. I would dream about what the future held for our family here.

As I was waiting, I looked up and saw Sam coming down the stairs with an unrecognizable baby in his arms... except, this baby was not a baby anymore. That morning, Daddy took Ethan for his first big boy haircut.

As Sam left for his workout, I ate up the cuteness of Ethan's new super short hair and took my big grown-up boy to the play area. Ethan started playing on the slides for a bit before he made his way to the plastic blocks that fit together to create curvy paths, slides, dips, and stairs to walk and balance on. He climbed up on the blocks, turned to me, deliberately reached out his hand and said excitedly, "Mommy, hold on tight!" Although he had said this phrase to me in the past, it brought me so much joy that, although my baby was growing up, he needed his Mommy right by his side.

Despite his request of holding on tight, I took his hand loosely and started to gently guide him up and down and around the blocks. He didn't get too far along his path before saying, "No mommy, this way!" as he repositioned his hand and mine so that we both had a tighter grip on each other.

My heart skipped. Ethan was teaching me how to walk alongside him, tightly hand-in-hand, walking the path together. This gesture melted my heart and was one of those significant indescribable moments that, in that very instant, I knew I was never going to forget.

It was the sincerity and pure love and open trust of the gesture that seemingly only the simplicity of a child could give.

I think about all the relationships I have in my life. I think about my relationship with Sam, my family, my close friends,

friends that I tend to hold at a distance, friends who I'm yearning to go deeper with, people in my life that I haven't really taken the chance to get to know, people who I haven't talked to in many years, and people from all the different circles of life around me near and far.

It doesn't take much thought to realize that it is so obviously apparent that there is a vast difference between my relationships before these circumstances entered my life... and now, during the aftermath. Don't get me wrong, we have always had incredible friends and family in our lives, but maybe by Ethan's standards, there was too much of a distance, too loose of a grip.

Maybe we were being too passive, putting up too many boundaries, giving too much space, being too polite. Maybe we were too lazy, too selfish, or too scared to go deep and do life together... for real. Because now in the midst of disaster, doing life... for real... with others means getting messy, revealing our weaknesses, giving into fears, exposing our vulnerabilities, sharing our pain, not always being polite, not always looking pretty... being *real*.

There was a time I lived my life at a distance. Ethan said, "Mommy, hold on tight!" Our close friends and family selflessly chose not to go through this with us from a distance, but have held on tight to us as we have held on tight to them. The bonds that have grown and that are continuing to grow have become exponentially stronger.

The messy pain of walking this path of life together tightly, hand-in-hand can sting, but the blessings prove to be abundantly greater.

When tragedy struck, the pressure squeezed us in the palm

of God's hand. But right before His hand closed, there were people who grabbed our hands tight, feeling the pressure we felt along with us as we were all crushed in God's hand together. By the time He opened up his hand, we couldn't get away from the fact that we are imprinted in each other's lives, inside God's hand and on His heart.

Ethan says, "Hold on tight." We weren't meant to go through this life alone.

Go Deeper:

1. Are there relationships in your life that you have held at a distance?

2. What has gotten in the way of going deeper with them?

3. Who in your life, if they were placed in a situation of pressure and darkness, would you not hesitate to jump in with them? How would you jump in?

[seven]

LIKE DADDY, LIKE SON

June 17, 2012

The following blog entry was written for Sam in his honor, on Father's Day 2012:

Ethan and his daddy shared a companionship that was rare. They shared a bond that was sealed with a love that could not be broken. Much of who Ethan grew to be was enriched by the relationship they cultivated together. Much of who Sam is today results from the impassioned way Ethan poured joy into his life.

Ever since Ethan was born, when I saw Ethan's face, I saw Sam. I was not the only one. Everyone could not help but make it abundantly clear to me (with maybe a rare exception) that his little newborn face with the blue eyes, strawberry blonde hair, and fair skin was a spitting image of Sam.

Sam, on the other hand, has the audacity to say that newborns look like worms. You would think that his own son would have been an exception, but no. Thankfully according to Sam, Ethan grew out of the "worm" phase.

Despite their similar physical features, I did not only see Ethan in his daddy's face, but I always felt Ethan through the essence of who Sam is. Their big personalities were also one in the same.

When I think of Sam, I think of life. I think of passion. I think of talent. I think of this contagious enthusiasm that emanates from himself into everything and everyone he connects with or touches. I think of this extra cavity of space in his heart that God gave him to love and to give and to pour out to others.

When I think of Sam, I think of Ethan. So much of who Sam is, Ethan was... his love of living his life in every moment with a tenacity that ignited hearts. Whenever he did *anything*, he did it with a passion, whether it was coloring, "cooking," playing, talking, reading, building, button-pressing, "air drumming" to the music at church, dancing, high-fiving, basketball playing, hugging, and yes, even crying! He did it with passion, an awe and a curiosity for life and a desire to live it with joy and reckless abandonment. He most certainly played the drums with passion and subsequently was a reason why we had to resort to watching TV with subtitles.

In addition to Sam in Ethan's life, I am so thankful for his other father figures who molded him into who he was. Papa taught as he loved. Hours upon hours were spent teaching him one-on-one about the things in life that we take for granted— the birdies in the trees that fly away, the moon and the stars in the sky, the loud sound of the train, the falling rain outside the window. We caught on to the fact that whenever Ethan did or said something new we never heard before, nine times out of ten, it was Papa who taught him.

Gramps also taught as he loved, to my mother's dismay, in a more unconventional way (you have to know my dad as I can't quite explain the odd quirks of his delivery when communicating with Ethan.) Ethan, on the other hand, had no problem with Gramps' 'way.' He went right along with his style of teaching Ethan about Lionel trains, conducting experiments, counting numbers, and making silly faces.

And although the amount of time they spent together was minimal, I believe Ethan held an indescribable place in his heart for his great-grandfather, Pop-Pop, that I can't quite explain or describe. I know he felt the love that Pop-Pop had for him. There is no doubt about it. Ethan was blessed in this life. The amount of love that he experienced was abounding.

I am so thankful for the amazing father that Sam was to Ethan. I always knew that he had it in him to be one exceptional dad, but I never would have imagined at what lengths he would run, to what heights he would climb, always reaching far beyond what was required or expected of him as a dad, not out of duty or self-satisfaction of some sort of achievement or success as a father, but out of a pure love.

Sam loved Ethan with passion. And in turn, Ethan loved with passion. Ethan lived with passion.

It is so easy for that passion, love, and joy in us to be quenched that yet a child so easily finds expressible. We plug through this life and we experience hurt and abandonment and failure and rejection and loss and disappointment and betrayal, and all the suffering that hits us in this fallen world. It seems as though sometimes that joy we once had gets sucked out of us.

Have you found yourself quenched of this passion for life? I have found myself at different times *completely sucked dry.*

But what I was truly longing to be filled with, I realized, was a love and hope that was absent. Where people can fail miserably and hurt us, God reveals his ignited love deep within us. It's a love that knows no boundaries, a love that goes beyond all heights and all depths and all measures.

We just need to know Him. Pursue a relationship with Him, to discover this great love.

God has the power to touch our hearts with His love so that a fire burns in us. We don't have to just go through the motions lifeless and miserable. We can allow His fire to burn in us so we can live again, with a fervor, a purpose, and a passion.

Ethan was a product of this burning love.

Go Deeper:

1. Who was the most influential person in your childhood? Why?

2. What in your life are you most passionate about? Are you currently living out your passion? Why or why not? In what way can you download your passions into someone else's life?

3. What areas of your life are you merely going through the motions, lifeless? How do you believe God's love can ignite a burning fire in your heart so that you can live in purpose and passion in those areas?

[eight]

ONE, TWO, THREE... PLUNGE!

June 22, 2012

Humpty Dumpty sat on a wall. Humpty Dumpty had a great fall...

One... two... three... [blow in face]...

Plunge!

When Ethan was as young as six months old, we started swimming lessons together at a nearby swim club. I could not wait to give him the same experience my mother gave me when I was a baby. Although he had "swam" in a pool a couple times before, even when he was only a couple months old, I couldn't wait for him to start these classes and enjoy some Mommy and baby time together outside of our regular routine at home.

One of the exercises Ethan's swim instructor, Miss Linda, worked on with us was the underwater plunge. He would start off sitting on the wall as we would sing this nursery rhyme to him, just to make it fun. Then we would say, "One, two, three," so he would know when to lean into my arms into the water.

Right before dipping his whole head and body under the water, Miss Linda instructed me to give him a short and quick blow in his face. As I learned from this very important step of this exercise, babies will actually instinctively hold their breath as a reflexive response after blowing in their face. (Who knew?) I learned that Ethan was no exception.

I was pretty scared the first time Miss Linda explained what she wanted me to do with Ethan. *You want me to do what?* But I realized this experience wasn't as scary as I thought it would be, especially after I found that blowing in his face actually did work and that I was able to gently hold him and guide him through the water the whole time.

Ethan never really seemed to love this exercise, but it was something that he never avoided and always leaned himself off the ledge into my arms into the water after the count of three, sometimes even with a silly smirk. He always displayed a complete trust that Mommy was going catch him, bring him under into unknown territory, and pick him back up again.

He was a bit dramatic when he was able to take a breath again out of the water, eyes wide open, a slight look of panic or concern, a bit of coughing maybe, a rub of the eye, a few splashes, but then realizing that everything was okay and that the experience was actually fun and thrilling. It was something he was willing to try again.

When you think about it, it's pretty crazy the amount of trust Ethan placed in me as he scooted his little butt off that ledge into my arms each and every time.

When I take plunges in life, whether the cause may be pure darkness and evil, or whether it may be as a result of a poor decision, or if it is God Himself calling me into deeper waters, pleasant is not the most precise word. These unknown territories are beyond intimidating. Vision is cloudy, if not absent, there's no telling how long I'm going to have to hold my breath, and there's no predicting what life looks like when I come back up for air.

The most comforting thing to know is when we are forced to take the plunge, God can take the plunge with us. And not only does He take the plunge with us and carry us through to the end, He prepares us right beforehand. He breathes on us. His breath becomes ours. His breath becomes the faith and power that we need to survive through and overcome the depths of life.

For Ethan, it was an automatic response to hold his own breath and trust. For me, well... that's a different story... I wish it was always that easy.

My automatic response has been to thrash and gasp in desperation, to start trying to take my own breaths, and to futilely struggle to keep my head above water by my own strength. I've found in doing so, the more I try to grasp for control, the greater the probability that I choke and drown.

If only I always expressed the faith in God that Ethan had in me as he would willingly lean into my arms down into the plunge... every time. It seemed that the more he learned to trust me, the safer he felt knowing I wasn't going to abandon him and that he was going to be okay.

Although many hardships have preceded my present, I have never reached depths like I have today. As I reflect on the incident a month ago, I will never forget the moment in the "privacy room" of the ER. I sat there in a surreal daze staring hazily at the bookshelf in front of me and thinking that in one way or another, my life was going to change forever. There was no avoiding it. The plunge was inevitable.

Later that night when I was able to grasp more of reality, I realized I did have a choice. Take the plunge without God and risk drowning. Or take the plunge with God and expect comfort, power, and blessing. Was I going to plunge into the arms of God? I was clearly given this choice.

Very late into the night as Ethan was transferred to ICU and we were let into his room to see him for the first time after the traumatic incident, I felt drowned by emotions when I saw him lying there in a coma in the hospital bed—just about lifeless, yet innocent and beautiful—hooked up to every machine imaginable and attached to who knows how many tubes. I never thought I would witness anything this horrific with my own son.

It was then I felt God calling out to me as if to say:

"You are about to take the plunge. But I can plunge down with you. I will be your every breath. The water will be over your head. But I will carry you. And you can be at peace in my love. Together, we can swim back up to sunny days again. Will you choose to lean into my arms and trust me?"

It has been far from easy. The pain has cut deeper than I have ever experienced. There are moments I feel my heart has been crushed to pieces. But through this pain, I know that I am not alone and that He is going through it all with me. I feel His arms carrying me through.

Although I am even now feeling moments of God's joys and blessings all the while as I am plunging into the deep with Him, I am looking forward to the blessings when we come back up for air, blessings in this life and the life to come.

Go Deeper:

1. When have you ever felt like you were drowning in life, desperate to find a breath?

2. Have you allowed God to breathe for you in a plunge? If so, what was that experience like?

3. What kind of plunges would you allow God to take with you? What plunges would you hesitate to give God control and why?

[nine]

MOON, COME BACK

June 25, 2012

I'm going to have to warn you straight off the bat, that this post is most likely not going to end up fluffy and cushy as some of my others do. My mood is quite drab at the moment, and I feel like it is just as important for me to write in my moments of doom and gloom as it is to write in my moments filled with peace and hope. One goal that I have had for this blog from the beginning is for it to be absolutely real, and I need to pour out as much of my true self into each entry as possible. I hope I have achieved that so far. I'm pretty certain I have.

One of my clearest memories that has replayed over and over in my head since Ethan's passing, occurred one afternoon when he was actually yelling at the moon. I'm not really sure why this memory has stuck to me so hard. His plea was just that adorable yet that intensely sincere.

This past spring I became dissatisfied with our backyard situation. Now, I wouldn't necessarily call our backyard a yard. The 'backyard' space that we have is pretty much a deck that fits a good size table and chairs, a grill and a little bit of space to walk around. We then have about a twenty square foot space beyond that of mainly mulch, and at the time, a lot of weeds.

This past spring Ethan was neither a helpless turtleback baby nor one on all fours. He was a rambunctious toddler on his two feet with much energy to burn and curiosity to satisfy, and I dreamt of a backyard for him to run around and play. Up until this point, however, basically throughout the fall and winter, our back deck and mulch area became Bono's, place of... well, you know, excrement.

We made a big decision in the beginning of the spring to turn the mulch area into Ethan's outdoor play area. After wrestling with the decision, we realized it was a win/win/*win* all the way around. Yes, it was a heavy commitment (for us at least) to walk Bono three times a day, but it was healthy for us because we got the exercise, our high anxiety dog got the exercise, and Ethan got exercise, along with some playtime fun.

We spent a couple days in the early spring heat pulling up weeds as well as fixing up and cleaning the back deck, and we picked out a perfect playground set for Ethan at the toy store. The playset had a castle and pirate ship feel and included a slide, a "rock-climbing wall," a ladder, a telescope and some fun places to crawl through and hide. It fit perfectly in our space. We added his red and blue basketball net, a couple kiddie chairs, and a kiddie umbrella to the deck, and Ethan's outdoor play oasis was complete.

We were just as excited as he was. He loved playing outside

in this area that now became his. I'm not sure what he loved more, dunking his basketball in his basketball net and chasing the ball around, or standing up on the platform of his pirate ship playset, steering the captain's wheel and looking through his telescope. He would love standing on that platform looking into the sky pointing out all the birds in the trees, admiring the clouds, and calling out to the blaring choo-choo train that would roll by. Other times he would just stand up there, lean and cross his arms on the ledge, rest his cheek on his arms, and stare down at Mommy as he relaxed in the crisp, spring air in complete peace. It was in these moments I knew we made the right decision.

Papa was the one who taught him how to look into the telescope to see the moon and the stars in the sky. It was so adorable to hear him say telescope in his cute toddler voice, "Mommy, look in the tel-scope. See the moon an' the stars an' the sky!"

Most times we would be out there with him at dusk after dinner. He would always get so excited to see the moon and point it out enthusiastically exclaiming, "Moon! Moon!"

On one particular day, we were playing outside midday before his nap. As usual, Ethan was playing with his telescope and was intently scanning the location in the sky where he had seen the moon the night before, but he realized that the moon was gone. In the most impassioned and persistent way he started screaming, "Moon, come back! Moooon... come baaaack!!!"

He repeated this over and over again for the whole neighborhood to hear. Each time he shouted, his demand became louder and more emphatic. He seemed genuinely frustrated and annoyed that the moon wasn't listening and that no matter how loud he yelled, to his dismay, the moon would not appear.

How disheartening it was that, any way you look at it, his shout out to the moon was fruitless. The moon was not going to magically appear in the sky. No matter how much hope and faith Ethan had in his heartfelt request, the moon was not coming back. The moon was gone.

There is something about this trial in my life that has been so drastically and blatantly different from all of the past afflictions I've faced. Up until now, there has always been a hope to cling to... a prayer and a belief for a specific outcome, be it a hope of physical healing, a hope of overcoming, a hope of restoration, a hope for a provision, a hope for a particular blessing. Even when I felt God's silence during these low times in my past, there was always this promise to hold onto for the specific outcome that I knew that God was going grant me, a prayer that was to be answered. Much of these prayers pertaining to the above have already been answered and the ones that He hasn't answered, I am believing in faith that He will.

But, with Ethan, no matter how loud I call for him to come back, no matter how much fervency and hope I have that his smiling face will magically appear right in front of my eyes, no matter how hard I pray... it's all pointless.

I cannot hope and pray Ethan back into existence on this earth.

I've never experienced anything so terminal and conclusive... so truly final. As long as I live, Ethan is not coming back.

I realize time will mend the pain and I am believing for God to restore, redeem, and go above and beyond to comfort and bless us beyond our imagination (because I know from experience, that's just what He does when we follow Him.) But as long as I live, there will always be a degree of this longing and emptiness in my heart for Ethan.

That said, just as the moon eventually does return into the night sky after the day is done, I know that after a very long... long... period of patience, I will return to Ethan.

Until then, although our moments here on earth are just a tiny speck in all eternity, I will be waiting for a lifetime.

Go Deeper:

1. Have you ever experienced a terminal and conclusive event, one that will not change even with all of the prayer in the world? How did you feel?

2. Have you ever experienced a moment that has lessened your trust in God? Why do you feel the trust was broken?

3. Where do you initially lean towards during life's hardships—towards disheartenment or towards hope? What steps can you take to work on being intentional at choosing hope?

[ten]

LIVE LIKE A ROCK STAR

June 29, 2012

As I sit in his room tonight, memories flood my mind. Amidst the deadening silence, I hear a faint laughter. I sit in the rocker, my arms cradled, yet barren. I see a boy hugging his Mickey Mouse tightly, yet the picture is cloudy and blurred. How many nights I stood over a lonely crib anxiously awaiting his arrival while I carried him for what seemed like forever in my belly. A crib and a room that was once empty waiting for him to arrive into this world stands vacant once again.

I have no words tonight... only to say, "I... miss... my... son."

Being that my words are few, I want to share with you the message our pastor and close friend, Mark, shared at Ethan's

Celebration Memorial. His deeply compelling and dynamic words moved many hearts that day and it couldn't have been a more perfect tribute.

I'm Mark. I'm the Pastor of a church called The Journey, and I am Sam, Kristen, and Ethan's friend. For my small part in this celebration of Ethan's life, I want to tell the story of two people.

I know we are all very moved today and we are human, so we are also wondering, *what does this all mean? What does Ethan's life mean? And what does his passing mean?* We would like to know what it means to his family and we would like to know what it means to us. I cannot even come close to completely answering those questions in the next few minutes, but I do know that it does mean something, and I would like to try to help us see that.

There are two people I want us to think about this morning. The first of those is Ethan.

This hour of celebration and these few moments of my speaking to you today cannot contain the whole story of who Ethan was and what Ethan did. There are certain epic things that happen and certain epic lives that are lived that we cannot fully describe or explain in a few minutes. But I will try my very best to share with you what I do know to be true about Ethan.

Ethan's life was rich and full! We are hearing today about some of the adventures he lived out. But Ethan also did a lot of other things throughout his life. If they were all written down, I suppose the whole world couldn't contain the books that would be written.

The first thing you need to know about Ethan is that he was a son, loved by his parents, Sam and Kristen. They crammed so much into Ethan's short life, and through them, he experienced so much adventure and fun and love. They took Ethan skiing, because every one-year-old should know how to ski, right? They traveled with him and had photo shoots with him that would make any supermodel jealous. Ethan did more amazing things in twenty months than I've done in the last twenty years! This kid really was a rock star, and his parents are rock stars too.

Kristen knew Ethan was special. She kept all these things she knew about him in her heart and thought about them often. The night after Ethan went to the hospital, came after a morning when Kristen very intentionally rededicated him to God.

Sam loved Ethan and included him in everything he was doing. Everything. I was meeting with Sam on a day that Sam, Kristen, and Ethan were getting ready to go on a trip. Sam was in army general mode. I overheard him talking to Kristen saying, "Be sure we bring these certain snacks. We need to pack this extra car seat. Don't forget that we need four bottles, two pacifiers plus a spare and thirteen Tupperware containers filled with Cheerios!"

The next thing you need know about Ethan is that he left before the people closest to him were ready. Many of you know one of the miracles of Ethan's story. Last Wednesday night the doctors thought he had gone, but he came back to us so we could have four of the most difficult, but most remarkable days to spend around him. Still, he had to leave.

Those of you who are married can relate to it this way… Sometimes my beautiful wife takes a little longer to get ready than I'd like. So I'm sitting in the car while she puts the finishing touches on her hair and makeup, and sometimes I'm tempted to just leave before she is ready. I don't do it, because I like being married.

But maybe that was Ethan! He just couldn't wait for us any longer. So he left even though we weren't quite ready. And we are all working hard not to allow our hearts to be troubled, but to trust God.

Another characteristic about Ethan is that he had a way of grabbing your attention. He was impossible to resist. Even while he was sick, he was grabbing the attention of literally thousands of people around the world. No one in their right mind could resist him. Much of my time around Ethan was spent desperately trying to convince him it was safe for him to give me a high-five. He had bright eyes, a big smile and he gave us hope, all of us. And particularly those who knew him and believed in how special he was.

It really is a tragedy if you didn't know Ethan, because he would have grabbed your attention.

Another thing you need to know about Ethan is that he is in heaven. I remember when the doctor told us he was absolutely certain Ethan was in no pain and we were all so grateful. God answered our prayers and decided to heal Ethan completely, not just temporarily, but forever. And when we found out he was in heaven, we started thinking about what he must be doing. We don't really know what heaven is like, so we try to come up with images that help us understand it. The image that we keep coming up with is that Ethan is playing in heaven. What else could he be doing?

And finally, the last thing you need to know about Ethan is that he gave his life to rescue others. I sat down with Sam and Kristen at the hospital on the night Ethan passed. They asked me if there was any reason I could think of not to donate his organs. Then, in the middle of their weariness and suffering, they walked through the interviews and signed the forms. I didn't have the words then, but I just have one word now, "Wow." They loved Ethan so much that they gave him to other people. They loved Ethan so much that they gave him to us. They could have hidden in the hospital mourning alone, but they invited us to be with them.

Ethan rescued some of us from our selfishness and distractions last week. We might have felt like it was the wrong time for Ethan to go, but it was just the right time for others.

Here's what I know about Ethan and his story...

We can't shrink his life into a few minutes. All the books in the world couldn't contain it. He was a son loved by his parents. He left before we were ready. He had a personality that grabbed our attention. He gave it all for others. And he is in heaven.

Ethan's story makes us think today, doesn't it? It means something. You can't hear, see, and feel the story of Ethan without being moved to respond in some way. So that is what you have done... by being here, by pouring out your love on Sam and Kristen and their parents, by giving generously to help in so many ways.

All that said, we might think today is all about Ethan. But there is someone else I want to tell you about, someone who is very close to Ethan and who loves him very much.

Jesus.

What I am convinced of today is that you can't really grasp who Ethan was and is without understanding who Jesus was while he walked the earth and who Jesus is today in heaven. I don't know how much you know about Jesus, but there are a lot of similarities between these two very special people.

For instance, just like Ethan, these few minutes of me sharing with you this morning cannot contain the whole story of who Jesus was and the things that he did. There is a guy named John who wrote in the Bible, "Jesus also did many other things. If they were all written down, I suppose the whole world could not contain the books that would be written." (John 21:25)

Jesus, like Ethan, was a son loved by his mother and father, but he was also the Son of God. Luke writes about Jesus' mother, "Mary kept all these things in her heart and thought about them often." (Luke 2:19)

John writes, "The Father loves the Son and includes him in everything he is doing." (John 5:19 Message)

Sound familiar?

Jesus left before the people closest to him were ready for him to go. Right before he left, his followers were freaking out, thinking, *what does this mean? We're not prepared. This is not how we thought this would go down!*

So Jesus said in the book of John, "Don't let your hearts be troubled. Trust in God, and trust also in me." (John 14:1)

Jesus has a way of grabbing our attention. He is impossible to resist. In fact, I wonder how anyone in their right mind could resist Jesus! He is affecting even right now, millions of people around the world. In the book of 1 Timothy, the Bible says, "Our hope is in the living God, who is the Savior of all people and particularly of all believers." (1Tim. 4:10)

It's really a tragedy if you don't know Jesus because he would grab your attention.

Like Ethan, Jesus is in heaven. We don't know what it's like there, but he does.

And finally, like Ethan, Jesus gave his life for others. It says in the book of Galatians that, "Jesus gave his life for our sins, just as God our Father planned, in order to rescue us from this evil world in which we live." (Gal. 1:4)

Jesus was an organ donor. He gave his heart and life to purchase freedom for everyone at just the right time. God could have hid in heaven, but He loved us so much, He came and gave his Son for us so we could have a relationship with God.

Do you see why these stories can't be separated? Both are sons, loved by their father and mother. They both left before we were ready. They both grab our attention. They both are in heaven. They both gave their lives for others. And both of their stories mean something.

I don't think you can experience the story of Ethan and not do something about it, and I don't think you can experience the story of Ethan and not do something about Jesus.

Their lives were, and are, so connected. And our lives and stories are connected to Jesus as well. That is why today means something. Ethan's life meant something, and he reminds us that *our* lives mean something.

There is a scripture in the book of Hebrews that says:

Keep your eyes on *Jesus*, who both began and finished this race we're in. Study how he did it. Because he never lost sight of where he was headed—that exhilarating finish, in and with God—he could put up with anything along the way: Cross, shame, whatever. And now he's *there*, in the place of honor, right alongside God. (Hebrews 12:1-3 Message)

We're all moved today and we also want to know, what does it all mean? I don't know completely yet.

But here's what I do know… If you see anything remarkable in Ethan's story, in Sam and Kristen's story, in Ethan's grandparents' and family and friends' stories… it's because of Jesus. And I know that you can know Jesus. You can turn from a life without God to a life that, like Ethan's, really means something. A life that will have joy and pain, exclamation points and question marks, but will give you what Ethan had while he was here then, and what Ethan has where he is now.

Ethan gave us hope and so does Jesus. Let's celebrate both of them today.

Go Deeper:

1. Are you intentional in living life to the fullest? If so, what are some examples? If not, what prevents you from living life to the fullest?

2. How has Ethan grabbed your attention? How has Jesus grabbed your attention?

3. What is God calling you to do as you experience the story of Ethan?

[eleven]

DADDY'S A DISNEY FREAK

July 3, 2012

I had the perfect plan. Looking way back to my college graduation and engagement period with Sam, I get a kick out of what I had envisioned for my life and how it vastly contradicts what has actually transpired over the past ten years.

Even though I wanted to bear a child immediately following our dream wedding, Sam was wise enough to talk me into his two-year plan of waiting to which I begrudgingly agreed. (Looking back, there is no way that I, at the age of twenty-two, was even remotely equipped for the world of dirty diapers and sleepless nights of a wailing child.)

So we would wait the two years. In the meantime, Sam would start a business where we would be raking in the dough, of course. Oh, and during that time, we would also travel the world. We would move into a gorgeous, new, sleek and spectacular home that I would design from top to bottom and we would have two children. The first of which being a girl, so that I could live out my dream of raising a tutu-wearing, ballet-pointing little princess and dress her up in the cutest and most fashionable clothes from my favorite kid's stores. Then, approximately two years later, we would have a boy, just to get one of each gender in... the perfect family, right? They would be the perfect kids and grow up with perfect manners and lead happy, perfect lives and we would all live happily ever after and be one big, perfect family.

Okay, so let's snap out of fantasy world. I'm sure it's not a surprise to you that that's not exactly where life took us. Life hit us and it hit us hard. There were years of disappointments, turmoil, fears, hurt, anger, drama, frustrations. You know, life happened.

Along with a slew of other circumstances and health issues, my battle with anxiety was a huge part of those factors that held us back in very significant ways. Our worlds felt like they were spinning out of control on many occasion. Needless to say, we were really good at keeping our struggles and pain hidden from the world, which in the long run, although we had many friends, unnecessarily isolated us to some degree.

So much for the two-year plan. I wasn't emotionally stable enough to take care of anyone else besides myself. There was no way we were going to invite an innocent baby into the mix.

Just when I thought "baby" would never enter my story, I finally was able to get my anxiety under control. After seven-and-a-half years of life lived between the two of us and after a desperate cry and plea to God, I conceived and gave birth to Ethan Isaac, September 1, 2010. Incidentally, parts of the pregnancy and birth didn't even go as planned, but that is a story for another time.

It was on a ski trip that February during my pregnancy that Sam started planning Ethan's 2012 Disney trip. He was not even born, yet Sam couldn't help but control his impulses to begin conceptualizing and dreaming.

If there is one thing that most people don't know about Sam, it is that he is one of those… you know… How do I put it politely?

Disney freaks.

He talked me into a two week Honeymoon at Disney World and has since then talked me into three more Disney trips with no kids of our own. True story. I am still waiting for my trip to Hawaii.

I can attempt to give you only a picture of the magnitude of his obsession, but the extent of which would be hard to grasp in totality.

I will take a stab…

Sam could tell you the wait time of lines at any of the hundreds of attractions on any given day of the year at any given hour down to the minute (data collected from five different websites.) He could tell you how long you would wait at the Dumbo ride line on January 10th of 2013 at 10:23am. He could tell you the best seat at any attraction. He could tell you where thousands of the hidden Mickeys are located within the architecture of all of Disney World. He could tell you where every diaper changing station is located. He could tell you how many steps it takes to walk from Main St. USA to Splash Mountain (675). He could tell you the best view at any of the parks for any of the firework shows. He could tell you where the statue of Walt is in the park and where the statue of him is pointing and why. He knows the back story behind every attraction that the Imagineers designed. He can tell you the speed of every roller coaster.

As I am writing this, Sam is spewing out all of these facts to me and my cynical self can't help but quiz him on the speed of Rockin' Roller Coaster. His immediate reply, "57 mph in 2.8 seconds."

If you showed him a picture of your family anywhere in Disney, he would immediately be able to determine the specifics of your location and all of the attractions that surround you even if they are not in the picture. I dare you to try him.

You could only imagine the time, the passion, the love he started to pour out into planning this ultimate Disney World trip for his long awaited son. He literally worked on the trip every day on his laptop all the way up until the day he passed. Hours upon hours upon hours he spent researching, updating, dreaming, and creating the perfect Disney experience of a lifetime. It served as his escape to enter into his fantasy world at any moment of the itinerary and play out that particular experience with Ethan... what they would see, feel, hear, smell, and taste together.

Thankfully, he kept most of this project hidden from me and didn't talk about it too often because he knew how sick I would become of hearing about Disney for two years and the plan that would be revised a million times in between.

Our trip was planned for September 5th to the 12th of 2012. We were planning on celebrating his second birthday at Chef Mickey's, a character breakfast including the Fab Five— Mickey, Minnie, Goofy, Donald, and Pluto.

Along with Sam's dreams for Ethan to become an incredible musician and to take what we both are best at and do all of those things better, Sam's most tangible dream for Ethan was only five months away. His dream that Ethan would come face to face with his favorite character, Mickey Mouse, and his dream to experience all the joys that the wonderment of Disney would bring, was right around the corner.

Out of all the questions I have regarding Ethan's passing, I have such a hard time grasping the timing of it all. It is so hard to accept Ethan had to leave us before Sam was able to live out his dream of him meeting Mickey and experiencing all that is Disney. A huge part of me hurts so deeply for him.

Sam had to endure the cancellation of this trip this past Tuesday, and he said that it was by far the hardest thing he has had to do thus far... harder than choosing Ethan's burial outfit and more heart-wrenching than choosing his gravesite.

As the woman on the other line went about her business in her jubilant Disney way, she asked Sam the reason for the cancellation. The woman was shocked at his answer and needed help from her coworker to continue to do what she needed to do amidst her sobbing disbelief.

It doesn't seem fair. We can painstakingly plan our lives out and attempt to control every aspect of it. But in this world of darkness, it is hard to explain all of the horror and unspeakable injustice that occurs all around us. We cannot begin to know or give answers to... "why?"

What I have come to know is that God wants us to be molded throughout this life into the person He has called us to be... to love others as we love ourselves. What would we appreciate? How much capacity would we have to love others? How many people would we impact if we just used the easy button in life or made our own selfish plans for our own gain?

I have always held a picture in my mind of God's dream for my life, not necessarily only what I would possess or do, but of who I would become. My insecurities, fears, distractions, or pride would always seem to get in the way of the person He has called me to be.

Now that I have been clinging on to Him in surrender, I finally have a taste of God's purpose in me. I finally feel like I am free to live out His plan, placing my trust fully in Him. What do I have to lose now? As Ethan has moved on, my heart has changed like it never has before.

One thing I do know is that God's plans for our lives are motivated out of His unconditional love for us. God's plans for us are perfect. God has the amazing capability of turning curses into blessings and working out all things together for good. He makes beauty from ashes and redeems the most horrific situations when we trust Him. The ultimate redemption was Jesus Christ crucified, our ultimate hope for peace, joy, and love experienced throughout all eternity when all tears and sadness will be wiped away.

Never in a million years would I have imagined this would be the path of Ethan's life. But Ethan is now in a beautiful place where he will never experience sorrow or pain.

They say Disney is "the happiest place on earth." Ethan is now experiencing the happiest place in all the universe...

Heaven.

Go Deeper:

1. What are some of the dreams in your life that didn't quite turn out as you expected? Have you found yourself questioning God as to why those dreams haven't been fulfilled?

2. In what way has a disappointment in your life led you to a deep internal strengthening and growth opportunity?

3. Are you willing to trust God to make beauty from ashes in a particular situation you have walked in or are currently walking in? What are the steps you need to take to walk forward in faith to give Him the reigns?

[twelve]

CELEBRATING ETHAN ISAAC

July 6, 2012

As I sit admiring the beautiful views of our towering vacation home overlooking the sea crashing into the rocks and cliffs below, I can't help but be so thankful for the blessings that God has showered over Sam and I, even during this deep loss in our lives. Making memories and being around our incredible family, in nowhere else but Puerto Rico, is just what we need to bring back some sunshine and joy into our lives.

Today, I wanted to share with you the eulogy that Sam spoke during Ethan's celebration service. It seemed impossible that he would be able to get through such an insurmountable feat, but he was able to communicate with grace and a strength that could have only come from God:

Today I will attempt to do what at first, seemed impossible. I will attempt to eulogize my son, Ethan. Once

I began to reflect on what I would say, it became very clear that the tone of this eulogy was going to be one of celebration and not remorse. But you know me, I always have a contingency plan. So, standing next to me is one of my closest friends, Jeff, who loved Ethan very much. If I'm unable to get through this, he's ready to jump in and see it through.

Kristen and I had been wanting a baby for quite some time, but the obstacles of life got in the way for years. Through much prayer, God heard the desire of our hearts and on a December morning, Kristen ran into our bedroom to give me some news. It was very early so I was still very much asleep.

"Uh, Sam?" she whispered. "Uh, Sam?" she exclaimed louder. Not sure what she could possibly be asking me at six-thirty in the morning, I turned half asleep and asked what was wrong. "Uh, Sam? You need to look at this!" I noticed now more alert, she was holding a home pregnancy test that read positive. I jumped out of bed overwhelmed with excitement, checking the test to make sure we were reading it correctly.

We were having a baby and couldn't be more excited! We agreed that we wouldn't mention it to anyone until we had visited a doctor and confirmed the results. But you know me, I can't keep exciting news to myself. So.... I told a ten-year-old drummer. Not a drummer who'd been playing for ten years, but a ten-year-old drummer. You see, during the day, Kristen and I continued to call and text each other like two little kids, and by the end of the day I was giving my last music lesson to my friend, Max, a ten-year-old drummer. As I watched him play his drums, I immediately began to fantasize about how I hoped to teach my unborn child my passion for music someday.

I turned to Max and said, "Hey Max, can you keep a secret?"

He turned back and said, "Yeah, what?"

"Dude, my wife and I are having a baby!"

Completely unfazed and partially unimpressed he turned back and said, "Cool," and went on playing.

I knew then that my preference was to have a boy, a boy who would someday play drums, a boy who would someday become.... my little rock star.

We named Ethan after a furniture store as we read the sign of Ethan Allen on Rt. 22 in NJ. But Isaac is a different story. In the Old Testament of the Bible, Abraham and Sarah, with heavy hearts asked God for a son, and when they received him they named him Isaac because he brought laughter and joy into their lives.

As soon as Daddy's little rock star, Ethan Isaac, was born, he wore AC/DC and Beatles onesies. We even created a playlist for him to fall asleep, full of lullaby songs by bands like Coldplay and U2 and, yes, even a "Twinkle, Twinkle Little Star" rendition by Metallica. Grammy was... concerned... to put it mildly.

As Ethan continued to grow, I could sense a passion for music that he clearly was starting to display. He would always be filled with excitement to hear me rehearse on my guitar. During our trips to the music store, he would make sure to get a good bang or two out of every bongo. While watching me play in the band at our church, The Journey, he would air drum along with us. And one of his favorite pastimes towards the very end of his life was to pull his

drum set (which weighed more than he did) right in front
of the TV and ask me to turn on the music channel so he
could play along to Maroon 5, his favorite band.

But he wasn't just a student of music, he was a student
of wonder. All that made it into his hands was always being
closely examined and taken apart. He had a true curiosity
for how things worked, tasted, felt or heard. He wasn't just
interested in watching the motorized car roll across the
floor, he would flip it over and try to figure out how to
assemble and disassemble the battery compartment. He
wasn't just interested in the light, he was also interested in
the switch and to our horror, how the lamp plugged and
unplugged into the wall. That is how his beautiful mind
worked. He was the perfect blend and the perfect balance
of emotion and intellect. And when he combined those two,
he was a force to be reckoned with.

For a boy that was only twenty months old, did he
experience life. We travelled with him on his first road trip
to Rhode Island at two months of age with our dog, Bono.
We took him for his first time down the slopes on skis last
December at our favorite ski resort. We had a blast flying
cross country to LA a year ago to meet his cousin, Lukey,
where we were able to experience Disney Land together
(not to be confused with Disney World.)

He lived.

He's my son so I get to brag a little... He took
swimming lessons and swam underwater at eight months.
He was the youngest member of his soccer club in the
toddler division. He had a vocabulary of over 300 words,

was starting to conjugate verbs and spoke Spanish. The Spanish can be attributed to his grandparents, Mama and Papa, and boy, did he love Papa. His Spanish was so good that his English was starting to gain a Spanish accent, especially when he would ask for one of his favorite snacks, "Coo-kees."

Just two weekends ago we took him to the National Zoo in DC with his best friend, Eli. His eyes filled with amazement as he saw large fish swimming in the fresh water tank at the Amazonian exhibit. Kristen and I take comfort in knowing that he made the same face when he saw Jesus for the first time. And as he stands in his presence, he must be saying his first words, "Light, light!"

On Wednesday night, I think I may have confused Ethan. After arriving to the ER and after being worked on by the trauma team, Kristen and I were pulled into a waiting room to be told that Ethan's heart had stopped.....that Ethan had passed, and that there was nothing the doctors could do. I immediately ran into the trauma room where I found Ethan's naked body on the table. I grabbed him by the arms and said "Ethan, you're a little scrapper, you know how to fight, so fight for Daddy. You have to come back, Daddy says come back!" In that immediate moment his heart started up again. I think the confusion for Ethan was that as he was making his way to Jesus, he heard my voice calling to him. His mind full of wonder was probably attracted to the beautiful light of God, but the loving boy he is came back when he heard me.

At that very moment, Ethan's ministry began. I didn't see it then but it can't be any clearer now. The mobilization of prayers throughout the country and the world unified an entire global community. Social media exploded! My analytical mind can't help but wish for an algorithm that could measure how many people connected to God through Ethan in prayer. From Nepal, to Holland, Japan, California, Puerto Rico, Texas, and many other places, thousands were praying. And they were posting and texting and calling.

And just as Jeff stands next to me today, your prayers supported us when there was no way we naturally could.

Ethan started something big. A friend of mine who I hadn't seen or heard from in over twelve years wrote to me saying, "Sam, I haven't spoken to God in over ten years, but today I spoke to God because of Ethan." Others wrote saying, "I am hearing God louder and clearer in my life than at any other time." And others expressed, "Ethan has restored my faith in Jesus."

It's so ironic that as people prayed for a miracle in Ethan's life, the miracle was actually happening in theirs, in my life, and in yours. Some of you may have never met Ethan, but all of us met God at some point last week. I will never forget what Ethan has done to my life. Never forget what God did through Ethan in yours. That will be his legacy forever. A short life of twenty months that ministered to more people than some have in ninety years of living.

To our family that jumped in the car first and then called when you heard the news of Ethan, I don't even have words, except ... I love you. To our church, the Journey, I am standing amongst saints. To all of our friends... the emails, the texts, the calls... Your support could be felt at three in the morning when our strength would fail us. Thank you all!

"For I know the plans I have for you," declares the Lord, "plans to prosper you and not to harm you, plans to give you hope and a future. Then you will call upon me and come and pray to me, and I will listen to you." (Jeremiah 29:11-12 NIV)

Go Deeper:

1. In what ways do you wish you could experience more out of life?

2. What do you desire to be said of you when your time here has passed?

[thirteen]

BABY DO IT

July 12, 2012

If there was one characteristic I admire about Ethan that was so blatantly clear he possessed, it was his fierce tenacity. True, his determination had caused much frustration for Sam and I, and sometimes imminent danger for Ethan. I always knew that down the road that drive would serve as the force behind anything he would want to accomplish in life and the dreams he would want to fulfill. It was clear that nothing was going to get in his way.

Along with this drive, he would express such focus during his efforts to complete the task at hand and nothing, not even a forceful "no," was going to stop him. He would get quiet and deep in thought and scrunch up his face. You could see his little mind racing. His mouth would gape open as if the wider he opened it, the more it would increase his ability to perform.

One activity that he loved to do (that Mommy and Daddy did not love) with his beloved drum set besides actually playing it, was to disassemble its parts.

His drum set consisted of a snare, a tom, and a cymbal all connected by metal frames that would attach into small holes on the bass drum. Each time Ethan took apart his drum set, it was not because he wanted to make a mess or be destructive, rather it was for the mere challenge of putting it back together again—and his belief that he could do it. He would exclaim…

"Baby do it!"

For Ethan, taking the pieces apart was a breeze. It was the reassembling that was a lot more challenging and required much more skill and patience. He would display such incredible amount of focus, relentlessly attempting to fit the heavy and wobbly pieces back into each of the holes of the bass drum. Being that the pieces were so big and his hands were so tiny and shaky during his attempts, he would eventually get tired and frustrated and ask Daddy for help. Daddy would get in there and guide his hands. And Ethan would get right back into it by himself, his mouth open wide in strain and concentration. He pushed forward intricately fitting the remaining pieces in hopes and belief that he would be able to once again play his drums and achieve his goal, his ultimate prize... until he disassembled it again.

Last week, Sam and I had the unforgettable experience spending a week in Sam's birthplace, Puerto Rico, with his siblings and cousins and their families. We shared a house near the beach that had breathtaking views of the seascape below.

We had the chance to embark on many an adventure while we were there, whether it was climbing El Yunque Rainforest, going rock-climbing on the shores of Pirates Cove, or snorkeling from one island to another off the coast of Fajardo.

I will never forget the memories we shared with the people we love and bonded with over the course of this past week. I don't think they will ever know our gratitude and love we have for them in the midst of our heartbreak, but we sure did share some fun and adventurous moments together.

My most favorite memory of our trip was climbing El Yunque with four of our more adventurous family members. I almost didn't even end up going. That morning it was downpouring, and hiking cold and drenched surely did not sound like a fun experience to say the least. I definitely went into it with a bad attitude and decided to go, caving into peer pressure that in the end, I am so grateful for. As we entered the national park and started driving up the windy roads of the rainforest, our ears popping from the elevation, my negativity began to fade and I started to feel pumped and excited about the journey ahead of us.

Our walk started out easy, the path was paved and thankfully it was only raining lightly, the forest serving as a canopy that prevented us from getting soaked. At this point, there were many people enjoying the beauty of the rainforest's waterfalls, the sounds of the Coqui's (frogs which are the official mascot of Puerto Rico), and the lush and fragrant greenery all around. Being that Sam's naturally athletic brother was leading out in front, we were moving at a very quick pace leaving other groups behind us in the dust.

Except for the necessary potty break and brief stops for photo ops in admiration of the waterfalls gushing down below due to the heavy rainfall, we took little time to catch our breath. To me, it seemed as though we were trying to beat some sort of world record for fastest time to reach the peak of El Yunque. The higher we climbed, the steeper the path became, the rockier the road, and the less people there were along the way. At this point, we had been hiking for an hour or two. I realized that I didn't even bring any water for myself. I only had one (amazing strawberry-banana) pancake for breakfast hours and hours earlier, and on top of that, the energy bars I brought for myself I had left in the car. Despite the lack of fuel, I continued onward with a smile on my face and a boost in my step.

At one point when we were all tired and hungry, we came to our first crossroad where we had to make a decision. The map along our path showed that there was 0.8 miles more to go until we reached the top. We were already tired and we could have very easily given up and started our descent back down. As a team, we all decided that we would push on forward, and what was another 0.8 miles? We estimated it would take us a mere twenty more minutes to walk those last 0.8 miles due to our obvious superior levels of athleticism exemplified by the fact that we were passing everyone. *Psshht... easy!*

Well, an hour later of hardcore climbing up rockier terrain, slipping in mud and splashing in puddles, each wishful bend in the trail that would possibly lead us to the finish line kept deceiving us. Despite Sam's repeated, "We're almost there," realistically, there was no end in sight. Negative thoughts started entering my mind, and before you knew it, I was starting to feel miserable. My legs ached. I was hungry and thirsty. And yup, I started my complaining and expressing my misery to Sam.

We entered another crossroads. We stopped. We came together. I said a prayer to myself. My greatest complaint was hunger and that I thought my legs were going to fall off. Other people felt shaky and others breathless. We all agreed we were maxed out beyond capacity.

Though, we had a decision to make. Were we going to give up now after hours of climbing, possibly right before reaching the goal, right before reaching the reward? Were we going to continue beyond our physical capacities and risk injury, risk being stuck overnight, and living out an episode of Survivor? Were we going to muster up the endurance and the determination and use what I've known to be the strongest muscles of the body, the mind and the heart, to get us to the top?

We all decided that there was no way we were going to quit after coming this far. We decided to dig deep down and trudge on forward. It turns out we weren't as maxed out as we thought we were. Maxed out of our comfort zones, yes; maxed out of survival mode, certainly not. We all split someone's energy bar, having just a bite each, and took a couple swigs of water we also had to share.

I have to say that all of us adventurers, looking back in retrospect, talked about the uncanniness of how far that small bite of energy bar took all of us. We went forward with a renewed determination and a stronger belief and desire for the prize that would await us at the end of the journey. This belief and desire would bring us through the physical discomfort to our end goal.

Okay, I have to stop here.

Literally as I am writing this (to be honest, I didn't really know where this post was going), God is revealing so much to me through this El Yunque adventure. It absolutely parallels my spiritual journey with God in ways that I hadn't taken notice of before tonight.

Since deciding to put my faith in Him over thirteen years ago, my journey with God has been, at many times, an arduous climb. At first the path was paved, the burdens light, but as time moved forward, my faith kept getting more and more tested. Little by little as my faith was tested, I began to gain endurance which allowed me to walk through and overcome the rockier paths, greater obstacles and steeper climbs. I've come to a few very significant crossroads in my past where I felt like I had lost all stamina and strength to continue following God. Endless disappointment, fear, and frustration made me feel like I was running on empty and there was nothing left in me.

I've found that I reach these important crossroads when I feel I cannot take anything more life throws at me and there is nothing left in me.

Do I choose the road that leads to defeat, or do I choose the road that leads to the reward? Do I choose faith?

Do I choose the *action* of *walking* out in *faith*?

That is where "Baby do it" comes in. It is a faith and a determination in *action*. Sure, God gives us the grace to fulfill His calling on our lives and He can serve as our help and energy boost like the energy bar did on our climb, but God cannot work in my life unless I *choose* to first take one foot and put it in front of the other... and then take another step... and another.

It wasn't hard for us to believe that the reward was there. The prize of the spectacular views and feeling like we were on the top of the world was awaiting us ahead. But we would not magically be transported there. We had to put one foot in front of the other, take one step and another step.

We stared down the obstacles. We chose the reward. We refueled in power. We stepped out in faith.

Now that's not to say it was a breeze the rest of the way, because that next twenty minutes of our climb was not a pretty sight. For me, it was keeping my mind focused on the reward that kept me going. And was it a reward! After one last steep climb up a paved hill and a long spiral staircase up a tower, we met breathtaking beauty, and the satisfaction of reaching our goal brought us great joy and fulfillment.

I believe that God has so many blessings that await every person who chooses to follow Him in the adventures of life. A lot of times the journey is far from comfortable and sometimes unbearable. Running on fumes, God refuels us with the power of His love. Then, it is our choice to step out towards the direction He is calling and the promises that await us around the bend.

My uttermost, deepest motivation in this life is to meet Jesus and for him to say, "Well done" (Matt 25:21) and to experience the treasures and blessings He promises. I now have a new motivation and a new drive to live my life in faith out of my love for God, knowing that Ethan will be one of the biggest blessings awaiting me.

Go Deeper:

1. In what areas of your life do you feel like you are running on empty? How do you allow yourself to be refueled?

2. What kind of forks in the road are you standing in that currently requires a decision to move forward or turn back? In what way does the prize motivate you to keep going?

3. What are the specific steps you need to take to move forward towards the prize? What hesitations prevent you from stepping out in faith towards the reward?

[fourteen]

MESSAGE IN A BOTTLE

July 12, 2012

Besides our excursion and climb up to the top of El
Yunque rainforest in Puerto Rico, Sam and I embarked
on another adventure later on in the week. This
expedition was completely inspired by Ethan, as if our trip to
Puerto Rico would not have been complete without fulfilling
this mission.

I started thinking about writing a letter to Ethan when a
friend encouraged me to make sure that I spent a little time
during the vacation talking to him in reflection and meditation.
This awakened my idea of sending out written messages in a
bottle to Ethan that Sam and I would individually compose.

It was last Sunday that we spent at the tropical resort where
we got engaged in Fajardo. Its beach is located on Palomino
Island about four miles off the coast, accessible only by ferry. It
is an oasis of its own and was the most beautiful beach we

visited during our stay. About a third mile off of Palomino Island, exists another very small island called Palomanito.

We had snorkeled from Palomino to Palominito a few years ago and decided it would be the perfect location to cast out our message... except that we failed to recall just how challenging this undertaking was. It was not just a hop, skip, and a jump to the island, contrary to what we remembered.

As soon as we set foot in the water, Sam spotted a shark swimming right along the edge of the water. *Perfect!* The shark was only a couple feet long and I'm sure not harmful, but *still...* talk about stepping out in that faith and determination that Ethan had always possessed.

"Baby do it," we seemed to have heard him whisper as encouragement for us.

Nothing was going to stop us from accomplishing what we set out to do. It was almost as if this was one of the major reasons we were supposed to visit Puerto Rico, to meet Ethan in a place out of which his roots were born and also in a place as close to paradise as our human minds could comprehend, the nearest place to where he now dwells.

We stepped out into the stony sand of the waters, slipped on our flippers and masks, and swam out in faith, committing to the task at hand while praying and trusting we wouldn't come across danger lurking in the water.

The swim was no joke. As we made it farther out, the shallow water covering the reef and full of colorful fish dropped off a ledge into a deep expanse of open waters.

There was no turning back now. The island that once seemed within our reach felt farther away than it ever had as we kept swimming and kicking without feeling like we were making any progress. I felt a loss of breath through the snorkel which kept causing me to stop, attempt to catch my breath in a bit of panic, tread some water, and continue on in faith. I could start to feel the sun's rays beating down on my back knowing I would no doubt end up with a sunburn. Although, I wasn't too scared of getting eaten up by sharks, I sure was looking out for them and praying to God that we would be okay.

After what seemed like forever, we finally touched land on Palominito, and unfortunately since we only had another half hour until we had to return our snorkel equipment, we couldn't take the time to relax and reflect. We had to push forward.

We decided against throwing the bottle from the island but to start swimming further out into the ocean to create a greater chance for the bottle to make it out to sea as opposed to being carried back into shore by the current and waves.

Sam was a bit edgy and frustrated because his mask was fogging up. We were emotionally and physically drained. We finally stopped and chose a place to throw the bottle where we could stand on a reef in the now very choppy waters, white caps surrounding us, and pulling us back and forth. Sam pulled out his bottle, a water canteen with "Ethan" in big bold and colorful letters, our notes stuffed inside. Through tears and deep emotion, we called out to Ethan and expressed to him how much we loved and missed him. We both kissed the bottle, and Sam threw it out as far as he could. We stood there on the reef for a few seconds as we tried to keep our balance amongst the wavy current, and we watched the bottle float away. In a stir of emotion that I can't quite explain in words, we grievously put on our masks and started our return trip. I turned back around to catch one last glimpse of the bottle as it drifted out further into the horizon.

Upon our return, the waters were choppier and heavier, and small waves were crashing over us. We felt a bit more desperate during our return, a bit more agitated and flustered from what we just went through, and the sight of a large sting ray caused us a bit of a concern immediately thinking of the Steve Irwin mishap years ago. Thankfully, we finally made it safely back to shore. We accomplished what we were supposed to do and it felt good in a bittersweet kind of way.

That night, from our bedroom overlooking the black abyss of the ocean, I pictured our messages in the bottle out there floating somewhere. I think that was part of the reason it was so hard for me to leave Puerto Rico. It was almost as if I was so scared to let Ethan go, like I was leaving a piece of me there, and where I was headed home, he would not be awaiting my return.

Who knows where the bottle is now or where it will end up. I just pray to God that He will, by His power, relay these messages to Ethan:

My sweet baby Ethan,

How do I begin to express in words the loss of letting you go? It is like a piece of my heart, a heart that continues beating on for you, has been ripped away. I am so grateful you will never ever experience such pain. Jesus has taken you out of a world of brokenness and has brought you into a place of endless beauty and light. While I wait a lifetime here before that sweet and precious day I get to cradle you in my arms again, I

promise you that I will not let you down here on earth.
Just as you love and follow Jesus and have made
Mommy and Daddy so proud, I want to make you
proud.

God formed and created you out of a love that is
so strong, I cannot even fathom. He made you special.
And you did not disappoint. You lived your short little
life as an example to the world. You shined your light so
bright that God is able to use you in ways that make
people live as they've never lived, laugh as they once did
when they were little like you, and love by a grace that is
only given by God. Out of the gazillion people who have
ever walked the earth, not many grown-ups, sadly, can
die fulfilling this calling.

I know I will fail and fall along the way, but I
promise you I will continue the ministry in which God
started with you. I will follow Jesus in the child-like faith
you lived out every day. I will choose to laugh in the
midst of sorrow but cry when I need to cry. I will live
life to the fullest as long as I am here. I will love as God
has called me to love.

Ethan, you are my inspiration and God has used
you to change my heart in ways that you'll never know.
Thank you so much for loving me beyond what I
deserved to be loved. Thank you for forgiving me for
the mistakes that I made and showing me what
unconditional love was all about. Thank you for those
three sweet kisses, smack on my lips, you shared
moments right before you got sick. Though you never
said "I love you" in words, I know you were expressing
them in those kisses. Thank you for sharing the Mickeys,

hearts, hugs, and kisses in the sky as that helped comfort Mommy and Daddy and helped us believe you are okay.

Although I know Jesus was and is there for you, for me more than anything, I need to express to you how sorry I am for not being able to do more for you in those moments when you were sick as they were the scariest moments of my life. I'm sorry I didn't show you more calmness and comfort. I'm so sorry I was so helpless. I'm sorry, that in the midst when you partially snapped out of it for those few seconds and you reached out to me poking my eyes and mouth wanting me to do something, that I couldn't help you in any sort of way other than making a call. I'm sorry when you spoke your last word to me, "milk," that I was unable to fulfill your request. Even though, as tears run down my face writing this and the sting of thinking about these moments are almost too much to bear, deep down I know that although Mommy couldn't do much to comfort you, I know that Jesus was there.

I am so grateful for the time we shared together. Even though the first four months were a huge struggle for both of us, and sometimes you made Mommy crazy when you were a little tiny thing, I loved you more and more every day and the older you grew the more fun we shared together. I loved teaching you and witnessing that brilliant mind of yours. You truly were a brilliant little boy. I'm so thankful that even though you were so young, we were able to have fun together, joke around, have conversations, share stories, and experience life together because of your curiosity to live and learn. I'm so thankful for your passion and your personality that bubbled over and lit up the room.

I promise you wherever I go, you are with me. Promise me, Ethan, that you will never forget me. Live it up with Jesus in heaven, I have no doubt that you are, but please be waiting for Mommy and Daddy when we come back to you. I can't wait for you to share with us all your experiences up there. I know you will have lots of stories.

"Love comforts like sunshine after rain," is printed on this journal page. You are mommy's sunshine. I know your love and God's love will be my comfort during the time we're apart. Mommy finds much comfort in knowing our time spent apart will be nothing compared to the time we will be spending together. Keep shining, Ethan.

Twinkle, twinkle little star. How I wonder what you are. Up above the world so high, like a diamond in the sky. Twinkle, twinkle little star. How I wonder what you are.

Much love and kisses,
Mommy

• • •

My Son Ethan,

Words will never be enough to express to you how much I love you. You are my world, and with your loss there have been times where my world has completely crumbled. I know this feeling will become better with time, and it helps to know that you are in a better place, but I still miss you.

I've had dreams at night where you've held my cheeks and kissed me on the lips just like you did to wake me up in the mornings. I hold all of your memories close to my heart... the ones we shared with Mommy and the ones only you and I shared together.

I pray at times to God that he would do me the favor of delivering a message to you, letting you know how much I love you.

I am so proud to be your Father. You amazed so many people with your talents, your ability to learn, your passion, your beauty, and your huge heart which at such an early age understood love so well.

I now catch myself wondering why I was so lucky to be your Father. You changed my existence when you came into my life. I am a better man because of you. Please help me continue to do that. I like who I was when you were around. Your Mommy needs me to keep being that man. I was called Sam all of my life, but when you called me Daddy I felt full. Complete. Whole. With purpose. I want to remain that way. I need to remain that way. I will see you again. Please don't forget me 'til that day comes. I am completely in love with you.

Now and forever,
Daddy

Go Deeper:

1. How has love comforted you like sunshine after the rain?

2. If you could write a letter to someone in your life as if it were the last thing you would communicate to them, who would it be and what would you say?

A LIFE LIVED IN BLACK AND WHITE IS DRIVEN BY FEAR. A LIFE LIVED IN COLOR IS DRIVEN BY HOPE.

#LESSONSFROMAROCKSTAR

[fifteen]

CRAYOLA 64

July 16, 2012

On the first day of school when Sam was in the third grade, every student received a list of school supplies their parents would have to purchase for the school year. On a very strict budget, his parents could not afford to buy him crayons. When Sam walked into his first art class, envious, he found that every last one of his schoolmates not only possessed a box of crayons, they all pulled out their Crayola 64 pack, the fancy one with the sharpener on the front.

When he went home to tell his mother, she visited a restaurant to ask if they would donate one of their packs of crayons. To his dismay, this crayon pack had three measly colors: red, yellow and blue. There was no way that his yellow could compare with the Laser Lemons, Goldenrods, Maizes, and other shades of yellow all the other children had in their 64 packs. He felt sad knowing that he could never draw to his full potential.

Ethan loved color. Initially his favorite color was yellow, or "wa-woe," as he first started pronouncing it. He would open his mouth exaggeratedly wide, drawing out each syllable. It was one of those responses that would make you clench up and spasm because the adorableness that oozed out through his words was so delectable that you just wanted to eat him up. At least, that was mine and Sam's reaction. We would coax him to say it again and again, just for that emotional high we would get from the almost unbearable level of cuteness factor.

Not only did Ethan love color and appreciate every color of the rainbow by name, he absolutely loved *to* color. I would have him sit on the floor of his room and place a bunch of coloring books and construction paper out in front of him. Sometimes I would only hand him two or three crayons to control the potential mess he would make on the carpet, but there was never any fooling him. He would scowl and stand up, reach up his hand pointing to his dresser and say, "More crayons, up there!" as if offended that I attempted to gyp him out of the full spectrum of tools he would need to create his masterpiece.

He would be so content sitting there adding one color upon the other, flipping through the pages of his coloring book, and coloring in the faces of every animal on every page. He loved when I colored along with him, not without him having control over which colors he wanted me to use, of course. He would ask me to draw pictures of different shapes, hearts, and faces just so he could color them in.

The life that Ethan lived radiated in color. If his life was a book, he splattered color and richness onto every page of his story.

There was no mundane in his world, no just getting by to make it through another day, no going about a life that was predictable and safe. He lived in the moment and recognized the beauty in the world surrounding him. He found excitement in spotting a yellow school bus, exhilaration in the sound of the choo-choo train, a joy in sensing the wind, curiosity to smell a colorful flower, and a thrill in tasting a lemon even though it made him wince and pucker. He was hooked on experiencing color through all five of his senses.

At different times in my life, I've found myself living in black and white. I've always been a person who easily finds boredom agonizing when caught in the vicious cycle of the monotony of life. I would imagine it's partly because I've been so blessed to have parents who have always made it a point from ever since I can remember, to encourage me to experience, to learn, to explore, to grow, to take risks, to feel, to smell, to touch, to taste the life around me. For me, lack of this enrichment in my life leads to, quite honestly, a depressing existence.

My biggest desire for Ethan was that he would grow up seeing the world in color. I wanted to raise him not to hide in the safety and comfort of black and white, but to experience the richness of color around him.

Color is choosing an item on the menu we would never normally try, as opposed to ordering the same old meat and potatoes. Color is doing a cannonball into the pool instead of tip-toeing in. Color is choosing a destination you've never been to before and trying to get there without a GPS. Color is having conversations with people who have different values, different backgrounds, and who look at life differently than what we know it to be. Color is listening to music that you normally wouldn't listen to. Color is starting a conversation with a perfect stranger. Color is giving to someone in a way that they could never pay you back.

The difference between living in black and white and living in color is that a life lived in black and white is driven by fear. A life lived in color is driven by hope.

Color is allowing hope to drive our decisions, not fear.

There are days after Ethan's passing when I have lived my life without color. Of course. It's the expectation of anyone going through grief and mourning. During these days and moments of deep pain, it is God who I have chosen to allow to color in my world of black and white. My life has been colored in with a hope that can only come from Him.

In Sam's situation as a young third grader, color came at a price. But it costs us nothing to add color to our lives. The only price to pay is having an open mind and an open heart. Once we open our minds, the colors are limitless. Once we put our fears aside, we can start drawing our masterpiece.

Go Deeper:

1. In what areas of your life do you see yourself living in black and white? What are your fears that are driving those black and white areas?

2. How can you splash hope and color into the black and white areas of your life?

3. How can God enhance and brighten color in your life?

[sixteen]

LOVE LIKE A ROCK STAR

September 1, 2012

Two years ago today, my beautiful baby boy, Ethan Isaac, was born! As I reflect back on that much anticipated day and on the sleepless nights, days, and weeks that followed, a deeper meaning of the word love was revealed to me, a love that I had never experienced so intensely before—a love given and a love received.

Love, a word that gets thrown around in the English language, has meanings attached to it that span a wide spectrum of intensity. The intensity of my love for Ethan grew deeper and deeper each and every day I had the privilege to get to know him and experience him on this earth.

We had a game the three of us played many mornings in bed after Sam had scooped him out of his crib to come and cuddle with us. We would say to him, "Ethan kiss Mommy," and he would give me a peck on the lips. We would say, "Ethan kiss Daddy," and he would give Sam a sweet kiss on the lips. However, he was not satisfied until Daddy and Mommy kissed each other. What brought him the greatest joy was to see Mommy and Daddy share love with one another. He would, with a huge grin and giggle, gently grab both of our faces with each hand and push them together so that we would kiss each other on the lips and do it again and again... and again.

Perhaps this was the greatest lesson of all, a lesson to love one another, to bring people together, loving others with no strings attached.

Although he didn't reciprocate love to me in the very beginning stages of his life, Ethan began expressing his love towards me in many ways, whether it was a silly smile, reaching out his hands for me to hold, handing me a toy, a display of trust, or a kiss on the cheek. Sometimes I didn't really understand why he loved me or trusted me... he just did... just because I was Mommy. I guess that was enough for him.

Thank God I wasn't supposed to be a perfect mom but a loving mom. But even in the loving mom category, I fell short many times.

Patience is a painful lesson for me, and I lack it often. It was not fun, but agitating, trying to get Ethan to eat a meal in his high chair as I'm trying to rush out the door. He would suffer the consequences of the blame even though it was my fault to begin with because I did not allot him the time I knew it was realistically going to take him to eat his cereal.

There were other times I took my personal anger and stress out on him by yelling too loudly or gripping him too angrily and forcefully. But time and time again, he showed that he so easily was able to forgive me and move on with his life, holding no grudges against me.

I did not deserve to be loved, yet he loved me. Ethan loved me with an unconditional love.

Why is it so easy for little children to know so clearly and to live out so strongly this no-strings-attached concept of love? Maybe that is the reason God loves children so much and calls us to live as little children.

I believe we are all called to love as Ethan loved— unconditionally.

God demonstrated this ultimate love for us through the sacrifice of his only son, Jesus Christ. The cross is a symbol of the ultimate sacrifice of love. Because Christ blamelessly died on the cross for the sins of the world and paid our penalty, nothing can separate us from the love of God when we believe in Christ and when we humbly enter into a relationship with Him... *nothing*.

We can try to wrestle our way out of God's love. We can turn our backs on Him. We can lash out in anger towards Him. We can commit disastrous sins. We can fail miserably. Yet time and time again, in the moment we turn from our sin and humbly come back to Him in repentance, He is waiting with open arms to pour out His love that never fails, a love that knows no boundaries, a love that not only covers our screw-ups but erases them forever.

God can express this love to us personally and does this, yes. But I believe another powerful life-transforming way His true love can be expressed is through *people* who *choose not to judge*, but to *love* those who *don't deserve* to be loved, those who have screwed up in reprehensible ways.

It is this no-strings-attached kind of love and forgiveness that puts on display the life-transforming power of the love of God lived out on this earth.

God *is* love. God's true love is powerful. This love literally transforms lives. It transforms hearts. God's love does not tear down and condemn. God's love builds up. God's love heals.

Unfortunately in the world today, people have much disillusionment towards God and Christ-followers, and for understandable reason. It makes me sad to see how God's love and church and the message of Christ is portrayed at times as a grotesquely inaccurate and distorted picture. It is so unfortunate because it prevents people from giving Jesus a chance and *truly* knowing him for who he really is.

I've seen a lot of judgement and pride, and self-righteousness projecting guilt on others because those people hold onto their own guilt. I've seen a lack of respect and lack of humility towards those whose belief systems don't line up with their own. I've seen closed minds and moral expectation placed on people who don't know Jesus. I understand some may read this and find my view controversial, but I humbly express to you that this is *not* the *love* Christ came to display. This is *not* the accurate depiction of the Gospel that I read about or, more importantly, that I've experienced in my life. (Can you tell I am beyond passionate about this?)

I encourage Christ-followers to *really* allow God to examine their hearts in this area of judgement towards those who don't have a relationship with Jesus. I will do the same for my heart; I know I have areas in my life that need to change. When I fall into judgement, I don't understand the love of God for myself, and I would rather hold onto the guilt. Instead of giving up the guilt to God and living freely, I project the guilt onto others.

It seems obvious, but please don't miss this: There is nothing more that drives a nonbeliever away from God than judging that person and expecting them to live up to our moral standards. I want to challenge myself to not just talk about how Christ loved, but live it for myself... *live* LOVE!

To those Christ-followers who live love out in their daily lives unconditionally, I encourage you! The power of the love of God being worked in you and through you is magnificent! Continue to be the light of the world. Continue to allow God to use you in the relationships around you to draw people to Him.

To those who don't have a relationship with God, who fell out of a relationship with God, or don't believe in God, and have been hurt or felt judged by someone who says they represent Christ, my heart hurts for you. This makes me so sad because it hits so very close to home. I pray that someone would reveal a no-strings-attached kind of love to you and that you would be able to see the power of God's love revealed through it. I pray you would realize that this condemnation is not the true representation of God's love, but that He ascribes unsurpassable worth to you, no matter how far you've fallen.

I, myself, am a product of God's love. I know firsthand what it is to screw up, fail, and crush the person I love most. Yet, because my sin is great, the greater I have experienced and seen how far God's love stretches. The God I know is not as portrayed in the condemning ways above. He is what is as described in this verse:

Love is patient. Love is kind. It does not envy, it does not boast, it is not proud. It does not dishonor others, it is not self-seeking, it is not easily angered, it keeps no record of wrongs. Love does not delight in evil but rejoices with the truth. It always protects, always trusts, always hopes, always perseveres. Love never fails.
(1 Corinthians 13:4-8 NIV)

Ethan didn't know a whole lot over the course of his twenty months of living on this earth. As any toddler, he was immature little person. There were a lot of needs that as his Mommy, I needed to meet for him and teach him to grow in. One thing he did know, however, was how to live out the most important command set out for us. He knew how to live LOVE.

He loved me beyond my faults. He loved me beyond my weaknesses and incompetence, when I had not a clue what to do the first week of his life in my sleep-deprived state. He loved me beyond my appearance at three in the morning or how beautiful or how *not* beautiful I sang to him. He loved me even after I endlessly ripped the things out of his hands and mouth that he would constantly want to grab and taste. He loved me even after saying no a million times to everything he wanted to do. He loved me on my fat days and on my bad hair days. He loved me when I didn't fulfill his happiness.

He loved me beyond my failures. He loved me beyond my anger. He loved me when I didn't live up to his expectations. He loved me through my sorrow and pain. He loved me when I was helpless in helping him in his seizure state by reaching out to me and touching me intently.

On this journey Sam and I are on together, it's as if in the remembrance of him, Ethan makes sure along the way to grab our faces and bring us together to love each other the way he loved us... even during the lowest moments of this most crazy week.

This morning, on what would have been his second birthday, we will visit Ethan's gravesite and release balloons in honor of his life as we will be holding on tightly to our very special friends surrounding us who have demonstrated this unconditional love to us. We are so very blessed that they would share the burden of this journey with us. We are forever grateful.

· · ·

I believe I have a story to tell, a story that isn't quite finished yet, and is still playing out as I sit here and type. I believe it will be a story of God's love and redemption and hope... I cannot wait to share it!

I believe that from sacrificial death comes life! I can't say I know why Ethan had to leave us, but I believe in the blessing of new life! I believe Ethan is happy and with Jesus. I believe God's work has just begun and His plan is unfolding. He has been more real now in my life than I have ever experienced before. I have hit rock bottom countless times in the past, but I can honestly say despite the circumstances, I'm not even close to that place. I am functioning in a whole other realm—in the hands of God.

My belief is more than a hope that I am merely clinging onto as a coping mechanism. It is real. I believe. Because God is real.

This is my last "Lessons From a Rock Star" blog post. I have found much healing through it and am so blessed to be able to express myself through my online community. I am overwhelmed by the impact it has had on people. Many have mentioned to me in comments, through social media, or in person, that I should write a book. Although a scary feat, it is my absolute intention to write a book entitled nothing other than, "Lessons From a Rock Star," and it is in the very beginning stages of a work in progress. I will use this blog as a backbone of the book.

Lessons from a rock star... these lessons were first, for Sam and I. Ethan, for the short time I was blessed to have him in my life, taught us lessons that I will never ever forget. They have changed my life forever. I am not the person I used to be as God has allowed me to see these lessons lived out through Ethan. It has transformed my life! I know what it has done for me. I now want to share the transforming love of God with as many as I can.

If this has touched you, please feel free to share this message of love with others and love others as Ethan loved!

He rocked our lives. He rocked our hearts. We will never be the same.

Go Deeper:

1. From your own experience, in what ways have you witnessed Christ-followers representing the love of

Christ? In what ways have you witnessed Christ-followers today driving others away from Christianity?

2. Why do you think it's so easy for children to live out a "no-strings-attached" concept of love? How can you express a "no-strings-attached" concept of love towards the people around you?

3. How has your knowledge of God's love transformed you thus far in life? In what way can a greater knowledge of God's "no-strings-attached" love towards you transform you on an even deeper level?

PART 2

THIS IS NOT THE END

TRAGEDY IS NOT WHERE
WE END, IT IS WHERE HE
BEGINS.

#LESSONSFROMAROCKSTAR

[seventeen]

THIS IS NOT THE END

Five years later, I sit here and read my heart poured out, through to the end. It's something I've only done a handful of times through the years. My lessons from a rock star. The glory of God oozing through every hope-infused word. Not my message but His message, learned from such unexpected pain seems so unfathomable, given to us out of His love to deeply touch those affected by Ethan's story.

It has been a mind-blowing five years of pain and love, ups and downs, healings and failings, obstacles and overcoming, reflection and revelation. A transformation in me and my life that, in awe, I stand struggling to comprehend.

I can't help but look back and remember a week or two after Ethan's death huddled on my bed grappling with overwhelming agony and heartbreak. I aimed to physically bring my arms together to hold onto something, frantic to grasp at what was merely a desolate space of air. With each attempt I felt my heart shattering into smithereens as I realized my motherhood had vanished alongside Ethan. There existed no baby to fill my arms.

Even in remembrance of all of this, when I look back at the last five years of my life, all of what I now see is the unmistakable, matchless, and undeniable beauty and love of God that He expressed to me, this broken vessel.

I cannot deny the massive transformation that has occurred and continues to occur in me, through me, and in the world around me. It's not that everything is ever perfect nor are the waters always crisp and serene. But it's that there exists a greater power now, stirred up within, riding the currents and waves alongside me. I have been positioned higher than I have ever soared before, as eagles fly with hawk-eye vision and clarity scaling the heights of the storm. At the same time, I've never chosen to position myself so low into the most honest surrender and humility. I do not deserve it, yet I am met with such unending love and grace. A transformative life continues to erupt as I see the hope that is in Jesus and access the treasures of the peace, joy, and love He promises.

I didn't always experience such beauty. The season in my life you would think I would express as "going through hell" or as a "dark night" was far from how I would describe the seasons following Ethan's death. Up until Ethan's time lived with us, a good majority of my adult life was riddled with "hell" and "dark nights," not necessarily circumstantially, but sourced from lies I entertained and fear that exploded in my mind. I had lived most of my life with grossly distorted vision, and it wasn't until after Ethan's death, my lenses seemed to slowly start coming into a greater focus.

My hope is that Part Two of this book highlights practical

steps you can take and, more specifically, choices you can make as you ride the waves of life. How does what should be labelled a dark night in your life transform into something so powerfully radiant? How can you see through a new set of lenses that will change everything? How can you, in the midst of the twists and turns and even tragedies of life, experience the peace, joy, and love God promises to you through the hope that is in Jesus?

CHOICE #1: I CHOSE TO BELIEVE THIS IS NOT THE END.

In my own words spoken in a video that was created for Ethan's first anniversary remembrance gathering:

> Since the beginning of this tragedy a year ago, we chose to believe that this is not the end. We chose to believe that we have a hope and a peace and a joy that goes beyond our circumstances. This is not the end of a hope of a family. This is not the end of our life and we're just looking forward to what God has for us in this life and the life to come, because we believe that this is not the end of our story.

> *This is not the end.*

Whatever you are facing on this day… this is not the end.

Have you lost something so precious that cannot be replaced, and you find it nearly impossible to take another step? This is not the end. Have you been crying out to a God you believe isn't even listening and therefore is hateful, hurtful, and enjoys witnessing the torment life throws at you? This is not the end. Have you been hurt and betrayed by those nearest and dearest to you? This is not the end. Are you plagued with the onslaught of lies that tell you that you are worthless and are a piece of garbage to be tossed out? This is not the end. Are you trapped in a dirty cycle of darkness that feels impossible to break yourself out of? This is not the end. Are you run down, bruised, shaken, utterly exhausted from striving to be something in this life with nothing to show for it? This is not the end. Do you hold a dream in the depths of your heart but at every direction you take there are roadblocks in front of you? This is not the end. Do you suffocate in a fear that paralyzes you and you cling to every shallow breath you can manage to find? This is not the end. Have you lost all energy and will to live? This is not the end.

Fill in the blanks with whatever you are personally going through right now...

This is not the end.

The lie wants to demand from you that all hope is lost. The lie wants to speak death into your soul. But what stands true for everyone who believes in the redemption of God and the hope that is in Jesus, is that this is not the end.

And not only is this not the end, if you choose this path, the most glorious, unbelievable ages are ahead of you in this life and the life to come, no matter what mess you find yourself in today. For tragedy is not where we end, it is where He begins.

I am and continue to be a testament to this very truth. I have been through every scenario described above at one point in my life or another, most of which happened before Ethan's passing. I have spent years at a time living in the pit of bitterness. In fact, it was my ever deepening bitterness towards God that would continue the downward spiral of the hell that was my life, or at least, that is the lens I saw it through. The truth was, I had a million and one things to be thankful for, but all I saw and received were the onslaught of lies that infected my heart.

Even though I couldn't admit it at the time, the physical ailments I personally suffered were in direct correlation to the fear and negativity that swirled in my mind on a moment to moment basis. So what I experienced for so many years was a nasty cycle of living in fear, leading to physical manifestations of anxiety, leading to debilitating physical circumstances, leading to bitterness towards God, leading to consummation of negativity, leading to physical manifestations of anxiety... And on and on the cycle continued.

Until, by the grace of God and choices I made to overcome the lies, that cycle of bitterness started to break down.

I had just found out I was pregnant with Ethan, and Sam and I were ecstatic. We spent a good seven years of our marriage childless even though I was desperate for nothing more in life than to be called, "Mommy." Not because I was unable to have children, as mentioned earlier, but we never tried because nothing was remotely stable in our lives.

Right around week six of my pregnancy with Ethan, all signs led to a miscarriage. I was even told by a nurse on the phone that I had, in fact, miscarried. Rage poured into my veins.

Only a couple weeks earlier Sam and I couldn't contain our joy and now this? How could God bless us with this incredible answer to prayer and then just steal it away from us, so cruelly and unjustly? Like a tease, dangling it in our face and then swiping it away when we tried to reach out and grab ahold of it, as if to say, "Psyche! Just kidding."

After all the times I shook my fist at God, when I found out about this unconfirmed but inevitable miscarriage, I never felt so much hatred and fury towards God. I didn't want to have anything to do with a God who willed downpours on my life day in and day out.

The rage that was bubbling up inside me surfaced and exploded out of every pore in a display of emotion that I am not much proud of. Blasphemous words, words that I had never used towards God, spewed out of my mouth so furiously that I felt like my vocal chords were ripping to shreds. I screamed out horrible utterances and told God that as long as I lived, I would never serve Him or love Him... ever... again.

I really meant those words when I spoke them. I sat there in the car as Sam drove me home from work where the perceived miscarriage happened. I tried fathoming what, logistically, a life looked like for me without God, being that the previous ten years of my life were consumed by a relationship with Him and serving Him in a church where we were heavily involved.

Thankfully, one of my very close friends at the time visited me that night and brought some light and faith back into my very dark picture. I made the choice to not give up, and I scrounged up every bit of hope that was left in me to decide to move forward and to trust God in the midst of my anger.

You can imagine my shock the next day as I braced for the impact of the inevitably fateful news. As I lay on the ultrasound bed after explaining to the technician what had transpired the afternoon before, she cheerfully responded, "Well, sometimes God works in mysterious ways because I see a heart... and it's beating! Do you want to see?"

I turned around in disbelief looking back at the monitor, and sure enough, there it was—a tiny little speck of a light blinking on the screen. It was the little light and life of Ethan, and he took my breath away.

God did not zap me to the ground with a lightning bolt because of the profane words that boiled out of my mouth toward Him the day earlier. Instead, He honored my honesty. God gushed out grace (that I clearly didn't deserve), and lavished over me the complete opposite of punishment— promise, joy, hope, life, blessing, and more love than I ever imagined He could give.

Something began to change in me that day. A lot of that bitterness I held in my heart dissipated and was blown off by the grace and love of God I welcomed in the midst of my ugliness and brokenness. Not that God had ever withheld His love from me, but the bitterness that I allowed to consume myself with and the false lens I saw Him through prevented me from experiencing the true love He had to give. I started to encounter the great power of His love. My receiving of that love began breaking every chain imprisoning me in the lie that rudely insisted God didn't care and wanted to see me suffer.

Shortly after Ethan was born and, shortly after I fought my way out of the postpartum that left me nearly nonfunctional on every level, I learned the power the mind has on the physical.

The more I filtered my thoughts and cast out negative thinking, the more I fell into a clarity of mind. The more I declared in my mind, or better yet and more powerfully, declared out loud, what was true and what was positive according to the Word of God, the more my fear diminished and the physical ailments attributed to anxiety started to subside. I do not take the credit for digging myself out of that pit, as God is the one who supplied the grace and performed the miracles; however, I held the brunt of the responsibility to choose to fight and to choose Truth and positivity.

It was only a few months before Ethan's incident and death that I finally received and accepted God's breathing of peace and joy into my life on a whole new level. I had never consistently relished in such overwhelming power of His love before.

Life was good. Life was more than good. It was fun and vibrant and adventurous. I began living through the eyes of my one-year-old, Ethan, growing more and more in awe of the little person, the genius baby he was.

To this day, the stark contrast between my reactions to the two separate times I lost Ethan (or thought I lost him) still floors me. The roots of those inversely opposing reactions has taken me years to bring into focus and dig up and comprehend. Because I spent a great amount of time and intensity reflecting and praying for clearer answers, the paradigm shift that occurred in my heart hasn't become as clear as it is now. I will continue to expound on this shifting that developed inside me in the chapters to come.

Ultimately, this shift led me to a new heart attitude, where

I realized that instead of expecting God to resolve my circumstances, I chose to purely invite God into them.

I realize it may seem like Part Two of this book is attempting to depict a formula of sorts. But I would like to stress that the points I am sharing with you are merely coming from my own experiences. Every person and situation is unique and because of that, I don't believe that there exists a specific recipe (outside of the Truth in God's Word) you can follow in a specific order to bring a specific outcome. This is not a recipe book.

That said, I humbly lay it all out there for you. You can apply as little or as much of the elements as you feel you need. And I believe once you start incorporating these shifts and choices into your life, you will be surprised what transformations you start to witness within you and around you.

Over the next few chapters, I will practically lay out three more life altering choices I made and continue to make in my life. I believe these principles lived out gave me access to the peace, joy, and love God had available for me during and following Ethan's death. My prayer is that it can offer as much power for your life as it did for mine.

The road you are currently walking could be the end to a chapter in your life. But I am certain it doesn't have to be the end of your story. Ask God to open your heart over these next chapters and humbly allow Him to speak into you in a way that may challenge your current mindset. Ask Him to reveal to you a new way of seeing life as you know it through a new set of lenses.

Go Deeper:

1. If grace is something given that is not deserved, how has someone else in your life, or how has God, expressed grace to you? How did that expression of grace impact you?

2. What is currently happening in your life that you could turn to and say, "This is not the end?" Do you have raw emotions you need to express to God in honesty?

3. What are the negative thought patterns (or lies) that run through your mind and discourage you into a doom and gloom mentality? What practical ways can you fight off those negative thoughts and fears and counter them with positive truths?

My Prayer:

God, I choose to believe, that no matter how bad my circumstances are today, that this is not the end. I believe that today is the dawn of a new day. Today is the beginning of a new chapter and my story has only just begun. I acknowledge those raw thoughts and emotions that I have towards you, and I open them up to you because I believe you honor my honest heart. I am sorry for the root of any bitterness that springs out. I give these raw emotions and bitterness to you laying them down before you. I believe in and am humbled by the grace you are waiting to pour over me because of that openness and humility. Help me to fight off the negative thoughts and fears and counter them with positive Truths you speak over me. Thank you God, for your faithfulness and for the opportunity I have to start fresh in a new day.

God's Promises:

We now have this light shining in our hearts, but we ourselves are like fragile clay jars containing this great treasure. This makes it clear that our great power is from God, not from ourselves. We are pressed on every side by troubles, but we are not crushed. We are perplexed, but not driven to despair. We are hunted down, but never abandoned by God. We get knocked down, but we are not destroyed. Through suffering, our bodies continue to share in the death of Jesus so that the life of Jesus may also be seen in our bodies.

2 Corinthians 4:7-9

So let us come boldly to the throne of our gracious God. There we will receive his mercy, and we will find grace to help us when we need it most.

Hebrews 4:16

"Lord, help!" they cried in their trouble, and he saved them from their distress. He led them from the darkness and deepest gloom; he snapped their chains. Let them praise the Lord for his great love and for the wonderful things he has done for them. For he broke down their prison gates of bronze; he cut apart their bars of iron.

Psalm 107:13-16

And we know that God causes everything to work together for the good of those who love God and are called according to his purpose for them.

Romans 8:28

[eighteen]

GOOD FATHER

Wednesday, May 16, 2012

S am stayed home with Ethan while I spent a full
Wednesday at work. Ethan was running a mild fever with
no other symptoms, so we weren't too concerned. I
called Sam a couple times from work to check up on him and
he assured me that morning he was high-spirited and vigorously
running around playing with Papa who came over for a visit.

By the afternoon, his fever went up again, so Sam gave him
some fever reducing medication. I told him that if his fever
continued into the next morning, we would call his pediatrician.

When I arrived home that night, Sam relayed to me that
Ethan was lazy in the afternoon, yet in good cuddly spirits. It's
not often that we had the opportunity to spend so much time
with him nestled and curled up on the couch together, being
that his energy level was always ramped up as you would expect
from any toddling boy. So, I took advantage of and lapped up
every bit of that sweet, snuggly time, and we watched some

"Winnie the Pooh" together. Then Daddy went to Pastor Mark's house for a special meeting that night.

Ethan was extra lovey-dovey as he simply relaxed there so peacefully, so content, smiling at his Mommy. At one point, a moment that took me off-guard, he glared heavily and lovingly into my eyes, his gaze piercing into my heart. It was a penetrating feeling I will never forget. He extended his head toward my face, puckered his lips and planted on mine a big sloppy, wet kiss. He had never really aimed with such purpose for my lips like that before.

To him, one kiss wasn't quite enough. He followed up with two more kisses smack on my lips.

Although he never actually said, "I love you, Mommy," I know without a doubt Ethan knew what love was. And I know that what he was expressing through those three sweet kisses was just that. "I love you, Mommy."

Okay. Pause. Tears are streaming down my face as I write this in disbelief. Even in this very moment as I type, God is revealing to me that those three sloppy, wet kisses were an expression of His love and presence over me, through Ethan, in His foreknowledge of the events that were about to unfold. It was as if heaven met earth through his kisses, just as a popular worship song exclaims. You may know it. Oh, how our Father loves us so much!

I cannot even contain the astonishment of His love right now as He has interrupted my telling of this story. I so irresistibly digress.

After finishing the episode of "Winnie the Pooh," I placed him into his high chair. He sat there in cheery spirits while I prepared dinner for him, but when it came down to eating it, he didn't have much of an appetite. After a long while of just poking and playing around with his food, I figured it was time to clean up.

For my own sanity of keeping him occupied and happy, I swiftly attempted to clean the kitchen before taking him upstairs for bed. We sang together as he stayed put in his high chair. I flit and floated swiping up messes and wrapping up food, dancing to place it all in the fridge (like any parent would do, right?)

Ethan filled in the words to the "Alphabet Song" and "Twinkle, Twinkle Little Star" like he never had before. I remember being amazed at what he was singing and thinking to myself how smart he had become. As he had picked up on so much just in a week, I wondered how much he would amaze me in the weeks, months, and years to come.

We sang "If You're Happy and You Know It" as I loaded the dishwasher, and he was clapping and nodding along. My plan was to take his temperature upstairs after I finished and then give him some more fever reducing medicine right before bed.

At this point, he was still content sitting in his high chair as I was completing my cleaning efforts of loading up the last of the dishes. I gave him a little treat of cranberries and white chocolate chips, but he seemed like he was starting to get sleepy, normal for this time of the night. In the past, in his cute way, he would stare out blankly into space, his eyelids droopy, and nod off into dream world. I thought nothing of his drop in energy.

Nothing prepared me for the horror that unfolded as I turned from slamming the dishwasher door shut and starting the cycle. I caught a glimpse of him staring into oblivion, food dribbling out of his mouth. At first glance, it crossed my mind that he had fallen asleep, but my gut told me something was terribly wrong.

At the sight of his body that now began to jerk uncontrollably, an overwhelming swell of fear flushed over me. I yelled, "Ethan! Ethan! Are you okay?" He gave no response, but to sit there blankly staring and jerking.

As I whisked him out of the high chair and started running down the hallway from the kitchen to the stairs, Ethan limp in my arms, I experienced a split-second encounter with God. He spoke into my spirit and I saw in my mind's eye, Jesus, and his arm outstretched saying, "You are not alone. I'm here. Do you trust me?"

In the next split-second as chaos of the emergency swirled around me, I made a choice rooted in the new-found joy that I was starting to cling to. I embraced the truth that He is a good Father by responding in my heart, "Yes, I trust you."

CHOICE #2: I CHOSE TO BELIEVE HE IS A GOOD FATHER

In a panic, I responded to the emergency by calling Sam and calling 9-1-1, fumbling around in distress until the ambulance arrived. Underneath it all, I held a deeply rooted assurance that everything was going to be okay—even as the situation continued to escalate at the hospital and was getting uglier by the second.

After such a long period of his unconsciousness, all I longed to hear was his cry, a cry that assured me he was going to be okay. I walked around the hallways aimlessly, from the trauma room, to the restroom, to the tiny, private waiting room, back to the hallways again. There were no cries to be heard, only the loud blaring code-blue alarms that did not seem to cease going off.

Standing there in the hospital hallway, I literally saw hazy white fog. The hospital personnel must have been fearing I was going to pass out because they kept suggesting I sit down asking if I wanted water. The only reason I finally drank the water was because of their insistence, not because I had any desire to fill myself with anything but the hope that Ethan was going to be okay.

Through all the haze and uncertainty, though, deep in my gut I believed God was with me. And I believed He was with Ethan.

As the doctors gathered us in the tiny waiting room to bring us news, Sam and I sat on the couch together anxiously awaiting what they were going to tell us. I tried convincing myself in a daze, that maybe it wouldn't be perfect news, but news that would assure us in the long run, this would soon become a distant memory. That this was a great scare, but Ethan was stable and was going to be just fine.

The doctor communicating to us sat directly in front of us, too close for comfort. Her expression was grave and heavy. When she spoke, I wasn't grasping her words, because they didn't make any sense. She spoke contradiction to my truth. She was saying that they spent a long time, a much longer time than normal trying to bring Ethan out of the cardiac arrest, but to no avail.

"Your son, Ethan, has died."

There are no words to describe these moments in time. You watch it played out in movies, or you view it happen in real life recorded on TV or online. You may imagine what it might feel like to be in that scenario of such sudden loss. But until you have lived it (as some of you probably have), you can't possibly know the feeling. I wouldn't even call it a feeling because there is no feeling present. It's a fantasy. A nightmare. But, most of all, a numbness. A disconnect from the tangible world around you. It's a state where your mind takes you to a nonfunctional place because if it did continue to function, it would be too much for your physical body to handle.

It was the very presence of God in the midst of our contradiction and confusion, I believe, that led us to run out of that room to Ethan in faith believing that this was not yet the end of Ethan's story. The power of God's present love, our love for Ethan, and Ethan's love for us, was what brought him back to life in those miraculous moments.

Although the doctors were dumbfounded, stating that they had never seen anything like it before and that they never tried so hard to bring a child back to life, I can't say that I was surprised that he miraculously came back to us. I don't know if it was the inability to accept reality or if really was actually my faith in God, but nevertheless, it's as if I expected the outcome of him coming back to life.

The assurance remained. I chose to believe that this was not the end. I chose to trust. I chose to believe my Father was good, no matter the circumstances that churned around me.

Yes, I moved forward in a haze of the unknown in all heartbroken delirium, but at the same time, in that moment I knew in the depths of my soul that my Father had my back.

That no matter what the outcome of this emergency was going to be, my Father was faithful, He was present, and He was working all things together for good. He was fighting for me. He was fighting for Ethan. I didn't have any answers or any capacity in my own strength. I just knew because I chose to fully surrender and trust God, that He would be faithful, for He is a good and perfect Father. I had seen Him move in my life in the past, felt His presence, and experienced His unmerited love, and this day was no different than any other day.

In the weeks to come, a verse in Jeremiah caught my attention and spoke to my heart. There were a few instances I saw it posted on social media and it appeared in cards and letters sent in response to our family's circumstances. It was also the verse that Sam shared at the end of his eulogy in my blog post, "Celebrating Ethan Isaac."

For I know the plans I have for you, declares the LORD, plans to prosper you and not to harm you, plans to give you hope and a future. (Jer. 29:11)

This verse evokes question and deeper meditation into the true heart and nature of God. It brings us to the heart of this chapter. It brings us to the very questions that you may be asking yourself about Ethan. It brings us to the very questions that you may be asking yourself about your own life:

If God says in His Word that His plans for Ethan are good, why did such a terrible event happen to such an innocent life? Did God create Ethan so that in His perfect will, Ethan would suffer and die so violently? And if God says that His plans for Sam and I are good, why was such a treasured promise ripped away from us?

145

Should we draw the conclusion that "everything happens for a reason" clinging to this ambiguous meaning and explanation of why? I can't tell you how many times I've heard this spoken from someone who has gone through a rough patch in their life:

"I failed my acceptancy exam, *but everything happens for a reason.*"

"I got fired from my job, *but everything happens for a reason.*"

"After dating my boyfriend for two years, the relationship fell apart, *but everything happens for a reason.*"

"My doctor found a lump in my breast, *but everything happens for a reason.*"

"My wife and I have tried multiple fertility drugs yet we are still unable to conceive, *but everything happens for a reason.*"

It is a popular cliché some affirm in our culture, but frankly I cringe a little bit inside when I hear it. I understand that it is a positive, "looking-on-the-bright-side" way of seeing an unfortunate circumstance. However, it is grossly limiting in that it steals from the true character and essence of who God truly is.

God and the universe that surround us are so much greater and infinitely more complex than what our finite minds can fathom. We cannot fully wrap our imaginations and limited intelligence around how this world legitimately operates.

In order to see God for who He truly is, in all of His greatness and all of His perfect love and glory, we have to in faith, detach ourselves from lies we are believing.

We have to stop believing the lie that says God is the one pulling all the strings. We have to stop believing the lie that says God brings forth sickness, disease, accidents, and death. We have to stop believing the lie that says all the bad things that happen in life are because of God.

If there is one thing that I have learned from Ethan's tragedy (although, obviously, I've learned so much more), I have learned who God is *not*.

God is *not* up there in the heavens writing out plans and destinies for one child to develop a life-ending cancer to result in one God-forsaken "reason" while another child is to grow up full and happy and healthy. He does not write plans for one baby to be miscarried in the womb for a "reason," and one to be stillborn because of cord strangulation for another "reason," and one baby to be born with no complications whatsoever. God does not write out the plans for one girl to be kidnapped into the sex trafficking industry for a "reason" and another girl to live a life of security and love with everything she could possibly need at her fingertips.

God does not, in His perfect will, write up these horror story plans for anyone that has ever walked and will walk the earth. He is a good Father. He is the perfect Father who writes up perfect plans for every single conceived life. His plans for us are not to harm us, but to prosper us, to give us a hope and a future.

God is also *not* a puppeteer. Our destinies are not fixed. He created beings in the heavens and humans on earth with free will. He is such a loving Father and so yearns to first and foremost have a relationship with us, that he doesn't force that relationship upon us. He doesn't beat us into submission to follow the good and perfect plans He writes up for us. He doesn't barge through the door that we have chosen to lock Him out of. We are not merely used as His robots, preprogrammed to walk out task after task. That is not a picture of a perfect Father. That is not a picture of a loving God.

Because of our free will, however, humans have become a fallen race. The Bible says we have all sinned and fallen short of the glory of God. We make terrible choices sometimes and think impure thoughts. That's not to say that all the unfortunate events that occur in one person's life happen solely because of their choices. Absolutely not! But just think of the incalculable number of choices that are made around the world on a daily basis, good and bad. It is mind-boggling, the complexity of it all, and how one person's choice during one moment of the day, effects another person's choice, which effects another person's choice. And so on exponentially. All of those choices are interconnected so intricately, much greater than our human minds can comprehend.

Another characteristic about God is that he is *not* a magician. He has the power to be, but in His perfect love, chooses not to be. I believe sometimes we expect God to wave His magic wand for us, and poof, in front of us appears an answer to every single prayer we pray without question. Although, I do believe God sometimes performs sudden miracles before our very eyes, which I have experienced myself, typically those answers don't show up so immediately. More often than not, answers to our big prayers come through a lengthier process of patience, contending, and consistent faith. We may have to go through a process of God digging up a root of darkness in our soul to prepare us to receive His answer and blessing. We may have to go through a process of being faithful by being patient for the right timing. Or we may have to go through the process of accepting that the prayer that we think we need answered is really not the best for us, and that God has something so much greater waiting in the pipeline.

There is no love in a magician god. For instance, a parent giving a child exactly what they want all the time, every time, does not cultivate depth in the child. In addition, a personal relationship cannot be developed without coming alongside that child during times of need. A magician god is merely a distant power standing high above you granting you what you want all the time, nothing more, nothing less. At the end of the day as His children, is this what our soul truly craves from a Father?

The truth of the matter is that we live in a dark world. There is a presence of evil that in this day and age is intensely difficult to deny. I don't have to go into details regarding the graphic imagery we have seen plastered all over mainstream media and social media outlets in recent years. Images of wars, disasters, terror, poverty, destruction, torture, hate, injustices, perversions, to name a few. The spirit of darkness exists in the unseen world around you and infiltrates the most innocent of people's hearts and minds. That presence, and that spirit, is the spirit of death, ruled by the father of lies. The deceiver schemes vicious attack on humanity day in and day out. This evil "father" plants lies in anyone who will entertain them. They are lies that consume the soul with fear and torment, and lies that falsely claim you are worthless, powerless, unforgivable, unloved, and all alone.

Simply put, man's free will combined with a spirit of darkness and mixed with some pure chance will generate atrocities that always lead us to ask the question "why?" Why does one child die from cancer and another one walks away healed? We could only truly know if we were God and could see the inner workings of darkness and light and everything that has gone on behind the scenes since the beginning of time.

So then, if we have settled in our hearts that darkness and free will of humanity are the culprits to the bad that happens in the world. If we conclude that God isn't the one who is pulling each and every string in your life that brings bad into it. We can now ask the question:

Who *is* a Perfect Father?

According to the Bible, the very Word of God, God is *the* all-powerful, all-present, and all-knowing being who lives in heaven. He has no beginning and no end. He is the same yesterday, today, and forever. In God the Father resides God the Son and God the Spirit. He is the triune God, "3 in 1." He is the great "I Am."

He is Creator of all things, in both the natural and supernatural realms. He holds all power over the cosmos and every living and nonliving creation ever created. He is the "strong force," physicists' official term for the undefined force that holds atoms together that cannot be explained. He is the very source and breath of life. In Him, we live and move and breathe. Because He so desired to share His great love with us through a relationship with Him, He created humans to inhabit and reign over the earth He created.

A good and perfect loving Father intricately knits together His children in their mother's womb in His own image. We are created into such complexity, a beautiful masterpiece He takes such unique delight in forming. By His grace He imparts power inside His children to move mountains in this world, not in their own strength, but through the power of the living God, the Spirit that resides in them when invited.

He is the source of comfort and security, bottling every single tear that we shed. After all, He calls us His children. He knows the number of hairs on our head. He grieves along with us in our pain, imparting encouragement and love, whether we know that He's there or whether we are falsely accusing Him of that very pain we are going through.

A loving Father creates His children and the inhabitants of heaven to have free will, so that they can choose on their own to unlock and open their doors into a relationship with Him. Out of love for us, He chose to take the risk that He would inevitably be rejected by many, in order to gain the love shared genuinely and openly by those who do choose Him.

A perfect Father is the essence of Love.

A perfect loving Father doesn't condemn or shame, but in His patience He pours out buckets of endless grace when we run our life into a downward, messy spiral. A perfect Father never abandons, never throws us away like trash to fend for ourselves amongst the oppressive ravages of this life.

When we put our trust in Jesus, there is nothing that can separate us from His love, no matter how heinous the offense.

No matter how heinous the offense.

Because forgiveness is always accessible when we choose to come to Him in repentance and humility. Our Father loves us so much that He paid the ultimate price. The price of sacrificing His only Son. A price worth more than all the riches on the earth and all the inheritance in the heavens. Your Father paid that price for you to save you out of death and darkness that is inevitable and to give you the free gift of everlasting life.

And that is the hope we have in Christ Jesus. Because Jesus defeated death on our behalf we can spend eternal life with Him.

Once we start to see God the Father as wanting all that is good for us, and we continue in our pursuit in getting to know Him in a deeper and greater way, a more glorious picture of God appears.

The truth of the matter is that the more you open your heart to the Truth of who He is, the more you start to see that God is greater and more loving and more perfect than your wildest dreams can comprehend.

By His sovereignty, He is my Creator. By His love, He is my Father.

Go Deeper:

1. What is your picture of a perfect father (human or as God)?

2. How do examples of human fathers (good or bad) complicate your view of God as a father?

3. In the past, have you ever tried to answer the question, "Why do bad things happen to good people?" If so, what was your answer? Does this answer portray God as one to blame?

4. What fears stand in the way of you believing there is a perfect, loving Father in heaven and that every single one of His plans for you are good?

My Prayer:

God, I choose to believe you are a good Father. I acknowledge that I have blamed you for things that the power of darkness may actually be responsible for. I ask that you would give me the courage to put the fears and lies aside that prevent me from seeing you as good. I pray that you open my eyes to the Truth of who you are and help me to experience for myself how much greater you are than the box the limits of my mind place you in. I believe that because of the access I have to you through the sacrifice of Jesus there is absolutely nothing that can separate me from your love, no matter how broken my past. I choose to pursue the knowledge of who you are and I believe that through this pursuit you will reveal to me more and more of the depths of your love. Thank you, God, that you love me beyond my brokenness. Thank you, God, for your goodness that goes beyond my wildest dreams.

God's Promises:

For this is how God loved the world: He gave his one and only Son, so that everyone who believes in him will not perish but have eternal life. God sent his Son into the world not to judge the world, but to save the world through him.

John 3:16

God's way is perfect. All the LORD's promises prove true. He is a shield for all who look to him for protection.

Psalm 18:30

For we are not fighting against flesh-and-blood enemies, but against evil rulers and authorities of the unseen world, against mighty powers in this dark world, and against evil spirits in the heavenly places.

Ephesians 6:12

Have you never heard? Have you never understood? The LORD is the everlasting God, the Creator of all the earth. He never grows weak or weary. No one can measure the depths of his understanding.

Isaiah 40:28

Keep on asking, and you will receive what you ask for. Keep on seeking, and you will find. Keep on knocking, and the door will be opened to you.

Matthew 7:7

And I am convinced that nothing can ever separate us from God's love. Neither death nor life, neither angels nor demons, neither our fears for today nor our worries about tomorrow—not even the powers of hell can separate us from God's love. No power in the sky above or in the earth below—indeed, nothing in all creation will ever be able to separate us from the love of God that is revealed in Christ Jesus our Lord.

Romans 8:38-39

He will cover you with his feathers. He will shelter you with his wings. His faithful promises are your armor and protection.

Psalm 91:4

BY HIS SOVEREIGNTY, HE IS MY CREATOR. BY HIS LOVE, HE IS MY FATHER.

#LESSONSFROMAROCKSTAR

[nineteen]

HEAVEN ON EARTH

Late that Wednesday night after Ethan miraculously came back to us, some of our close friends and family travelled near and far. They spent time with us standing by in the large waiting room outside the ICU. There was a profound sense of tension, exhaustion, and unnerving stillness that consumed the room. By that time it was around midnight and this uncharted territory of the unknown felt too much to bear.

That said, I was a bit more functional than I had been in the ER, a horrible shaken mess, but at least I was now coherent. I was absolutely dreading the moment a nurse would call us to walk into Ethan's room and witness him for the first time after this whole catastrophic event unraveled.

Alongside the dread of seeing Ethan so helpless and lifeless, oh how I longed to hold and cradle him in my arms and tell him everything was going to be okay. How I still hungered to hear him cry. Of all the times Ethan's incessant crying drove me up the wall, nothing in those moments would bring more music to my ears than to hear him cry again.

Finally, after what felt like an eternity, it was time to meet him in his room in the ICU. Sam and I anxiously stood up after a nurse called us out of the waiting room. I may have held my breath the whole way as we walked down the hallway. I don't think there was a moment in my life that the unknown ever felt greater.

As his door cracked open, nothing prepared me for the sight. At first glance, all I could notice was the floor-to-ceiling machine that filled the cold, gray, and lifeless room. There was a bed in the middle that extended out from the big machine. On that bed was Ethan, connected to every tube and wire conceivable.

He was lying there so peacefully. I don't think he had ever looked so angelic, his big blue eyes were restfully shut, his eyelashes spread across his porcelain skin. How was it that something so beautiful could be in such a dire state of being?

I did not hear a cry or a laugh or a murmur in those moments. Besides the whir of the machine and a beep here and there, all I heard was silence… a deadening silence that came from Ethan.

Yet.

In that silence, there was a still, small voice speaking so gently into my heart. It was the voice of God asking me to make another choice.

CHOICE #3: I CHOSE TO INVITE HEAVEN ON EARTH

I wrote previously about this choice in my "One, Two, Three… Plunge!" blog entry. In that post, I shared how I felt God speak to me about how I was in the midst of taking a very deep (and obvious) plunge. God gave me the choice to invite Him into the depths with me as opposed to taking the plunge alone. Would I invite Him?

My answer was an unequivocal surrender. I needed God to dive in with me as I knew from my past the exasperating feeling of gasping and treading water to survive on my own. This time, I knew I needed to avoid this strenuous unnecessary effort at all cost.

Very late that night after I was able to further process our new reality, I found it impossible to opt out of sleeping in the room with Ethan when given the option to sleep elsewhere. I don't know if I would actually call it sleep, however. I would doze off on the "bed" in his room for ten minutes here, twenty minutes there as nurses and doctors created a constant commotion, coming in and out of his room throughout the night.

The biggest torment of that night was waking up probably twenty times over its course, reliving the nightmare over and over and over again. Reality hit me every single time I awoke from consciousness, praying to God, yearning that it was merely a nightmare, and that Ethan was down the hall resting soundly in his comfy crib in the warmth of our home. The bed's metal springs jarring into my back, however, wickedly affirmed that this was not the case.

Thursday May 17, 2012

Despite a night of anguish reliving the terrible ordeal, one thing I did know, see, and feel the next morning was God's presence in that place. That Thursday morning when I awoke from the long agonizing night, I was confounded with the sense that angels had flooded the room. I cannot explain it in a way other than to say that I felt their tangible presence. In my mind's eye, I saw them. An incredible and unexplainable peace surrounded me as I felt the very presence of heaven here on earth.

As I look back on this experience, I see that my invitation was received when I humbly invited God down into the depths of these waters with me. Not only did God so lovingly show up, heaven came down to earth into the darkness of my nightmare and brought His light, hope, and power into it. Heaven came down in overwhelming love just like the kisses from Ethan that smacked me on the lips just the night before.

1. I chose to believe this is not the end.

2. I chose to believe that He is a good Father.

3. I chose to invite heaven on earth.

There was a peace and a love, yes, even a joy heaven brought down to us that week. I experienced heaven and never felt closer to eternity than I had before. It was as if God was hugging me and holding me and speaking continuous soft, subtle words of encouragement every time I breathed in and every time I exhaled out.

God knows me inside out as He does all of His creation. He knew what I needed to hear from Him. He knew where my focus needed to be in order for me to survive the week, and not just merely survive it, but come out on the other side with strength and vitality, as an overcomer.

God knew my weakness, that I didn't have the capacity to pay attention to anything that was going on in the physical realm with Ethan's condition. I cringed every time the doctors came into the room just because I knew they would spout off medical terms and scenarios and test results matter-of-factly coming from a world of logic and reasoning which, at that point, I wasn't ready to hear.

Ethan was a completely healthy child and then so suddenly his body failed him. It was hard for me to accept anything other than his complete healing. It was what everyone was praying for, what everyone was believing for. It didn't matter what the doctors said at that point because I was believing the God of the impossible, the God that could miraculously heal Ethan. I was living in a world of eternity held by God.

God knew for me, out of the weakness of my soul, the only world I was capable of existing in at the hospital with my deathly ill son, was my heaven-on-earth-world. Thank God for Sam's strength and response to emergencies. In complete opposition to my makeup during crisis, his adrenaline pumps into high gear, his mind and instincts sharpen with increased alertness. Thank God I could trust him to absorb the information that came from the doctors and to make any decision that needed to be made.

And thank God for our friends and family who came to visit us over the course of Ethan's time in the hospital. We felt heaven come down through them as well. There were moments of laughter and joy that cut through the tension we shared. They never left our side. We needed to laugh in order to stay sane, and I believe the laughter held healing power. Prayers were being lifted up every which way for Ethan's complete healing, and we received more and more support as each day passed. The outpouring and response from different parts of the world was a manifestation of the heavens opening up around us. We felt God's love expressed to us through all the support we received.

As I reflect on what it meant for me to invite heaven down to earth while Ethan remained in the hospital and the following days of grief thereafter, I can't help but meditate on how my prayers must have started to give off a different ring. I can't help thinking that the heart behind the prayers and the actual prayers themselves began to start shifting and transforming into a new prayer I wasn't used to praying.

When we as humans pray for any problem in life, and I don't think I would be assuming incorrectly, most of our prayers are solely focused on asking God to fix our problems. Which is fine. We need to continue to pray those prayers. But God refuses to merely act as a serviceman coming into our homes to fix a lightbulb, unclog a drain, or repair the oven when we call on Him, then walking right out the door moving on to fixing the next problem in someone else's life. Servicemen don't care about a relationship. They do a job, get paid, and leave.

Jesus gives us an example of how to pray in the book of Matthew. Chances are, you are familiar with the Lord's Prayer.

Maybe you know it by heart. The New Living Translation helps us think about this prayer in fresh light:

> Our Father in heaven, may your name be kept holy. May your Kingdom come soon. May your will be done on earth, as it is in heaven. (Matt. 6:9-10)

On earth, as it is in heaven.

May your will be done *on earth*, as it is in heaven.

Did you catch that?

Let's let that soak in…

Jesus is calling us to pray for the perfect will of the Father to be played out on earth, *just as His perfect will is played out in Heaven.*

I don't think I've ever grasped the meaning of this part of the prayer until this season of my life although I've recited it countless times. And while I never noticed how powerful those words were, I believe they are a form of what my once, "Fix-it, God," prayers have morphed into after Ethan passed.

Contrary to a diluted serviceman's subconscious view of God, the truth of the matter is that God's desire isn't simply to appear in the picture alone when we cry out to Him in times of need and then move on. He desires to bring the glory of Heaven down with Him—His power that doesn't make any sense to the natural eye. He desires to give us access to peace, joy, love, and the hope which is in Christ. He desires to bring the beauty of

His miraculous light and love. He desires to bring us everything that is available if we would only ask with surrendered and humbled hearts.

God's will for us is to taste heaven, even here on earth.

Do you dare believe that God is much more loving and personal than a serviceman? Do you dare believe that God is so much more beautiful and holds so much more glorious power for you than you ever imagined in this life? Do you dare pray for God to bring heaven's power down to earth over the situations in your life and believe He will?

What do you have to lose in asking?

Go Deeper:

1. Reflect on the Lord's Prayer, Matthew 6:9-10. Do you see those verses differently than how you've seen them in the past? How?

2. What is your idea of heaven? Have you experienced a glimpse of heaven on earth? What did that look like?

3. What fears do you have in inviting God to bring His power into your problems?

My Prayer:

God, I choose to believe that your desire is for me to experience heaven on earth. "May your will be done on earth as it is in heaven." I pray that you help me to see you as a God who is much more than one who can fix my problems. I give up my fears to you, those fears that prevent me from inviting you to not just fix, but to come down into my circumstances and move your power over them, alongside me. I open my heart up to your supernatural power in expectation that your desire is to perform miracles, that your desire is to speak to my heart when I come to you with a quiet spirit of humility to hear from you. Thank you for the peace, love, and joy you bring when heaven invades my world.

God's Promises:

For the Lord your God is living among you. He is a mighty savior. He will take delight in you with gladness. With his love, he will calm all your fears. He will rejoice over you with joyful songs.

Zephaniah 3:17

Such love has no fear, because perfect love expels all fear. If we are afraid, it is for fear of punishment, and this shows that we have not fully experienced his perfect love.

1 John 4:18

Those who live in the shelter of the Most High will find rest in the shadow of the Almighty. This I declare about the Lord: He alone is my refuge, my place of safety; he is my God, and I trust him. For he will rescue you from every trap and protect you from deadly disease.

He will cover you with his feathers. He will shelter you with his wings. His faithful promises are your armor and protection.

Psalm 91:1-4

Seek the Kingdom of God above all else, and live righteously, and he will give you everything you need.

Matthew 6:33

When you go through deep waters, I will be with you. When you go through rivers of difficulty, you will not drown. When you walk through the fire of oppression, you will not be burned up; the flames will not consume you.

Isaiah 43:2

I pray that God, the source of hope, will fill you completely with joy and peace because you trust in him. Then you will overflow with confident hope through the power of the Holy Spirit.

Romans 15:13

We know how much God loves us, and we have put our trust in his love. God is love, and all who live in love live in God, and God lives in them.

1 John 4:16

[twenty]

WORSHIP

Sunday May 20, 2012

The following is a social media update Sam and I posted the night Ethan died:

At 6:45pm Sunday, Ethan gave his life to save another. After a heart-wrenching day filled with a spectrum of emotions, we have been able to access an indescribable peace. He has been with his Heavenly Daddy in a place of perfect joy and happiness. We have come to realize that the miracles we have been praying for have been all of you. Ethan touched people's hearts and brought many together to the throne of God in prayer, some taking the step to talk to God for the first time in over a decade, others hearing God speak to them louder and clearer than ever before. If Ethan's experience has brought you closer to God, don't allow his passing to be in vain.

Continue to seek Him out with the same fervor you sought him out over the past five days. As far as the lives Ethan has saved, a few children will have a new heart, lungs and other vital organs Ethan has donated. Thank you all for your encouragement and support, for it helped sustain us during the darkest valley of our lives. Please continue to pray for the journey that lies ahead of us. We have never been so scared, yet we have every confidence that God's grace is sufficient.

I spent the afternoon coming to terms with such finality. After I experienced a feeling of spinning out of control when Ethan's blood pressure skyrocketed, one of the last indicators his body was about to completely shut down, we couldn't escape saying our goodbyes.

It actually ended up being a beautiful opportunity shared between just Sam and I. Before we spoke our last farewell, we smothered every part of Ethan's body with kisses and talked gently to it, telling him how much we would sorely miss him. I remember yearning to see his cute little toes one last time, so I removed the socks he wore that whole week and caressed and kissed them sweetly. There was a peace-loving presence that filled the room, and as burning as it was to blow him those final kisses as we departed at the last sight of his earthly body, we possessed such cherished assurance knowing he was in tender hands and that we would, on one glorious day, meet him again.

We then spent some time directly following our goodbyes filling out a multitude of paperwork and forms down the hall that would allow for Ethan's organs to be donated. I would have never imagined as I rushed into the hospital with Ethan on the ambulance at the start of this life-altering journey that only five days later we would be walking out those doors leaving his precious body behind. The feelings were surreal as Sam and I endured the long, somber walk through the parking lot in the dusk of the night. We entered our car and the harsh reality punched us in the face unapologetically. There was no evading the barren car seat behind us that coarsely reminded us Ethan's material body had vanished from our lives.

On our way home, we stopped for dinner with family and close friends whom we had gotten used to having around with us that whole week. That intimate hour at the restaurant was the beginning of my new life with Ethan no longer tangibly in it. My journey had only just begun.

I have to be honest and say, besides the gaping hole in my heart that had just appeared from Ethan's absence, I felt relief. I felt relief from living in the unknown of what was going to happen at the end of each day spent in the hospital. I felt relief from living in the unknown of what kind of news we were going to wake up to. And I felt relief from living in the unknown of what our lives were going to look like or could have looked like long-term. A relief knowing where he was and that he was in good hands.

One of my consuming thoughts that night was the fear about walking into a silent and desolate house. (Well, besides Bono who had been quite abandoned for a few days minus an occasional visit. Poor guy, he was clueless, though, as always.)

I remember on our drive home from dinner, as I attempted to comfort myself, I imagined the pain wouldn't be so bad. *Just how long is a lifetime anyway?* I had been so used to living in the clouds of eternity, clinging to the hope in God during the time spent at the hospital, that fifty or sixty years didn't feel too unbearably long in that moment in time. Did it?

Who could know the unimaginable pain I would have to endure the next few months that followed?

But who could have predicted the peace and the love and the moments of joy that would stream over me during those next few months, and that continue to pour out into this very day? Who could have imagined heaven opening and gushing out over us so we could taste it here on earth?

That fateful Sunday, I could never have imagined.

CHOICE #4: I CHOSE TO WORSHIP

Monday, May 21, 2012

The next afternoon we spent at The Journey. Sam was used to, in his leadership role at church, preparing and creating content for its Sunday services. He worked in his element with me alongside Pastor Mark, planning Ethan's celebration memorial service.

I am so thankful for that time we were given at The Journey. It helped focus our energy in a positive way as we used our creativity to produce a day that would celebrate and honor Ethan's life while elevating the glory of God in the midst of it all. I felt so filled to allow God to inspire us to design the day in the greatest redemptive way we knew how.

As we sat there during the planning meeting, I began to sense a deep desire wash over me as I felt my heart yearn to sing and worship during the service. Serving as a worship leader on the worship team in church is one of my biggest passions in life.

As I had the privilege of regularly serving in this area at The Journey at that time, it wasn't too far-fetched of an inclination.

If you are unfamiliar with it, worship as a part of church usually occurs at the beginning of the service. It serves as an opportunity to outwardly express our love and adoration to God for all He is and all He has done for us.

Worship, much more than a timeslot in a church service, can also be experienced one-on-one with God. Ultimately, it is an attitude of the heart. Usually expressed through singing and music, I've seen it equally articulated so beautifully through other creative outlets like dance, writing, and even through art and painting. No matter what voice the expression embodies, the most crucial condition to God is not the quality of the song, but the purity and surrender of the heart.

In the natural, leading a worship song during Ethan's memorial felt like a daunting task on so many levels, but my spirit yearned so passionately for it. Someone brought the same thought out in the open during this meeting and suggested it to me, and before my rational side could convince my heart it was a ridiculous idea, I said yes, absolutely yes!

That day, we organized a group of family and friends who were willing to help Sam and I fill in with instrumentation and vocals where needed, and we spent a good amount of time in preparation for the big day.

Wednesday, May 23, 2012

On the morning of what one would think should be deemed the worst day of my life by a long shot, I made another monumental decision added onto my previous ongoing choices:

1. I chose to believe this is not the end.

2. I chose to believe that He is a good Father.

3. I chose to invite heaven on earth, and

4. I chose to worship.

As I rode in the car on our way to Ethan's celebration service, my heart raced and my stomach began to coil up in knots again as I played out the day in my head. There was question from the other musicians as to whether or not there was time to practice our worship song before the ceremony. After all, the night before was spent practicing with all those involved. I was on edge and consumed with a paralyzing fear when we arrived to the church from all I was about to face that day. But I thank God for the opportunity I had to insist that we all, indeed, should do a run-through.

I needed to feel God's love. I needed my soul to be comforted and put at ease. I needed to be set free. I knew that worship was the key of release. You see, worship is an act offered up to God, but in that sacrifice of praise, God refills us with so much greater than what we pour out to Him.

Sure enough, by the time the song was complete, my declarations of praise to God brought power to my spirit. The light from the lyrics and outward expression dispelled any tormenting darkness and fear I sensed in the atmosphere and in my heart. As my voice sung praises to God during the mere 'practice,' my weakness and despair turned into peace and a lightness in my soul. It brought confidence and assurance from God that, yes, on a day that the ultimate dread is supposed to consume, I was given the ability and authority to tap into the peace, joy, love, and hope God had treasured and stored up for me.

By the time the actual ceremony began, we could sense heaven all around us. There were moments of laughter, moments of tears, and moments of power that splashed over the hearts of hundreds who were present. I believe the greatest power I personally experienced, power that I believe still reverberates through my life over the course of time today, is because of the worship to God that flooded out of my soul on a day that I naturally had no reason to be thankful.

Without a doubt, the effects of that power on that day and the days following are still felt on this day and every day.

During that season of serving on the worship team at The Journey, I led worship almost weekly. God knew how vital it was for me after Ethan died. Not that I needed to worship and sing on a stage; God knew the prayers and songs that were lifted up from my heart regularly to Him in secret. But there was something during that season about the open expression of worship alongside others, a declaration of joy and thankfulness offered up to God in unity.

There was supernatural power released on my life when I openly chose the opposite of how one would be expected to respond after loss. Since I, as a believer, had access to a strength of not mourning as the world mourns, and my dependence to move forward in life came solely from the power of God, God gave me the joy in my heart to genuinely stand up there and praise him with more passion and purpose than I ever had.

I often wonder what in the world people were thinking, especially the Sunday I led worship directly following Ethan's death. I remember distinctly how I felt, by the grace of God, so filled with joy and filled with His love to get up there and praise Him and sing with all reckless abandon in my heart. I must have looked delusional. Maybe some thought I was in denial.

Personally, I would have guiltily labelled someone crazy to be up there hands-clapping cheerful with a smile on their face only a week after their kid died! I could see myself falsely assuming they were merely going through the motions detached from their devastation.

But God knew my heart. He knew that out flowed a genuine expression and a pure adoration, versus a mere song I was singing. And because of that, I experienced a healing touch and the power of the presence of God, a taste of heaven here on earth. I learned firsthand that a song from the lips delivers melody and verse but worship from the heart delivers victory and joy.

I look back through all the years of my journey of my worship towards God. I realize that for so many of those years, I held such a shallow view. It was something that I looked forward to doing in a congregation, but when it came down to me living out a life of worship and thankfulness, I miserably fell short. Instead of being thankful for and focusing on all the good blessings God had for me in my daily walk with Him, I chose to consume myself with those things that were going wrong in my life. I did not realize the power worship had to not only bring the joy and confidence of God's love into my life, but also the power it had to change my very circumstances when offered up with a genuine heart.

After Ethan died, something deep occurred within me. It's as if choosing to worship through the deepest pain I had ever experience forced me to dig down into the uncharted territories and depths of my soul. That digging gave way allowing light to penetrate where it was never able to penetrate before.

My worship changed after Ethan died. In turn, worship changed me. Because I chose to open up unhindered in worship, the greater I have been able to experience God's presence daily.

I can't comprehend how I would be able to live without it now as it has become a lifestyle for me, the very source of my joy to go about my day. Not necessarily on a stage out in the open, but a practice I have learned to start my day in the moments of awakening. An attitude of thankfulness in my heart.

The Bible says that evil comes to kill, steal, and destroy our lives. Evil came to kill, steal, and destroy Ethan's life and the lives of those who loved him the most.

Evil assumed I would cower in despair and defeat, and curse God again like I did the first time when I thought I lost Ethan to a miscarriage. Evil assumed a chaos of destruction that would come upon our lives and my marriage with Sam. Evil assumed we would lose our friends and draw far away from family, continuing on in a numbed existence of trauma and bitterness towards God, the life sucked out of the both of us. All of these reasonable predictions do not deviate far from what the astronomical impact that loss like ours statistically proves true for others.

But I believe, because I chose to worship that day and the days to follow, power was released through the song in my heart alongside the rest who worshipped with me. A power and a confidence that is still felt in my life up to this day. A power that is alive and exists throughout the words and pages of this book.

Worship serves as a weapon against darkness in hard times. Choosing to worship through the darkest times in life opens the heavens to rain down power and light, dispelling darkness. Where blame expressed towards God feeds into that darkness, a stance of worship communicates and celebrates victory. The victory we have in Jesus.

Today I exclaim loudly these words for myself, promises that God has for all those who mourn:

"You have turned my mourning into joyful dancing. You have taken away my clothes of mourning and clothed me with joy, that I might sing praises to you and not be silent. O Lord my God, I will give you thanks forever." (Psalm 30:11)

Go Deeper:

1. What does worship mean to you?

2. If you attend church, what is the difference between your worship on Sunday morning versus your worship over the course of the week?

3. What are the areas of pain that exist in your soul that you have found it almost impossible to worship through? If light was able to penetrate through the

darkness of your pain through worship, how would you imagine your life or circumstances changing as a result?

My Prayer:

God, I worship you for the Truth of who you are. Help me to go deeper in worship towards you, that I would express my thanks to you not only for the good that happens in my life, but also help me to worship you through the hard times, knowing and believing you are faithful and good and are working to turn curses into blessings. I pray my worship goes beyond Sunday mornings and that you help me pour out a spirit of worship towards you throughout my everyday life. I ask that in the areas where I lack trust, you would give me the courage to worship through the deep painful areas of my life, that your light would penetrate into those depths carrying the healing power of your love. Thank you, God, for the healing you will do in me through worship and the joy and power that it brings.

God's Promises:

The thief's purpose is to steal and kill and destroy. My purpose is to give them a rich and satisfying life.

John 10:10

For the LORD your God is going with you! He will fight for you against your enemies, and he will give you victory!

Deuteronomy 20:4

177

The Lord is my strength and shield. I trust him with all my heart. He helps me, and my heart is filled with joy. I burst out in songs of thanksgiving.

Psalms 28:7

"But for you who fear my name, the Sun of Righteousness will rise with healing in his wings. And you will go free, leaping with joy like calves let out to pasture. On the day when I act, you will tread upon the wicked as if they were dust under your feet," says the Lord of Heaven's Armies.

Malachi 4:2-13

Always be joyful. Never stop praying. Be thankful in all circumstances, for this is God's will for you who belong to Christ Jesus.

1 Thessalonians 5:16-18

The light shines in the darkness, and the darkness can never extinguish it.

John 1:5

All praise to God, the Father of our Lord Jesus Christ, who has blessed us with every spiritual blessing in the heavenly realms because we are united with Christ.

Ephesians 1:3

Let all that I am praise the Lord; may I never forget the good things he does for me. He forgives all my sins and heals all my diseases. He redeems me from death and crowns me with love and tender mercies. He fills my life with good things. My youth is renewed like the eagle's!

Psalm 103:2-5

A SONG FROM THE LIPS DELIVERS
MELODY AND VERSE, BUT WORSHIP
FROM THE HEART DELIVERS
VICTORY AND JOY.

#LESSONSFROMAROCKSTAR

[twenty-one]

SEEING THE UNSEEN

"For our present troubles are small and won't last very long. Yet they produce for us a glory that vastly outweighs them and will last forever! So we don't look at the troubles we can see now; rather, we fix our gaze on things that cannot be seen. For the things we see now will soon be gone, but the things we cannot see will last forever." (2 Cor. 4:17-18)

How many times did I read this verse back in my younger years, a fear-filled and clueless young adult timidly stepping out into the "real world" post college graduation. Every single day I would walk through the doors of my new entry-level job, sit in my tucked away cubicle at the start of my day, and crack open my little blue leather covered bible. It was only a couple years at that point that I walked closely with God and believed in Jesus as my Savior. The fear that consumed me on a daily basis caused me to cling to my faith.

I would flip through the same old underlined series of passages every day for a year or more, even, and this verse in 2 Corinthians was one that I would read and reread over and over again. Back then I could not even begin to grasp its meaning even though it so profoundly intrigued my spirit.

First of all, how could God have the nerve to tell me that my present troubles are small? At the time, I lived my whole life in the imprisonment of my fear that consumed my mind. From one second to the next I was suffocated by it, and my faith was the only breath I felt could sustain me.

The world feels like it is crashing around me and God is telling me my troubles are small? How on earth am I expected to focus on something that I cannot tangibly see?

I realized that back then I saw things through such a warped lens, gravely distorting how good and perfect God was, the power He had accessible for my life, and how much He loved and longed to have a relationship with me. It took me too long to stop believing the lie of doom and gloom and start believing that this is not the end.

I had a lot of knowledge about God, sitting under much biblical teaching and Bible study. But it took years and years for me to live in the freedoms I live in today by trusting God's goodness enough for me to let down my walls with Him. I finally allowed Him to break those chains of fear I held onto so tightly. It took too long for me to see clearly enough to make the choice in faith that God is a good Father.

Because of my lack of sight and understanding that God doesn't just want to fix my problems, but his desire is to bring down with Him all the power of heaven, it took forever for me to experience the very breath of heaven as my source of life through its drowning currents. It took too long for me to finally make the choice in complete surrender to invite heaven down to earth and experience all the glory that comes along with it.

Because of my shallow view of worship and the potential its purest form had to transform and impact the atmosphere around me, I missed out on years of the glory and blessing God had for me through it. It took too long for me to finally choose to worship in purity from the depths of my pain.

After a slow process of coming to a greater comprehension of what it is to see the unseen, those days spent in the hospital with Ethan catapulted me into a greater understanding of this revelation that I experienced so acutely and remarkably.

I chose to believe Ethan's tragedy was not the end of our story, therefore, my perspective changed from shutting the book on our lives to simply turning the page into a new chapter of hope. I chose to see God as perfect and good and because I chose to invite Him to plunge into the waters in complete surrender, by nothing other than the grace of God Himself, I couldn't escape the perspective of the eternal that I experienced in the hospital.

By the grace of God, I couldn't escape the level of peace that made absolutely no sense. By the grace of God, I couldn't escape the saving hope I had in God's Son, Jesus, whom I had never met or seen with my natural eyes before. By the grace of God, I couldn't escape the intangible assurance that whatever did end up happening, we would at the end of the day, be wrapped in the loving arms of the Father in one form or another. By the grace of God, I couldn't escape the taste of heaven God brought down with Him. And I couldn't escape the beautiful sight of all of it.

My gaze was fixed on heaven on earth. My gaze was fixed on Jesus. Because of this, I felt eternity's embrace.

Ultimately, I did not see my lifeless son, I saw Ethan loved and held by Jesus. I saw Ethan alive. I see Ethan living today because out of Jesus' death, comes life. Eternal life.

That's why, after believing for the majority of the time in the hospital that God would work a complete miraculous healing in Ethan and when the news came on Sunday that he was brain dead, I accepted his death completely that very day. I accepted Ethan's physical death fully and clearly because my gaze was continually fixed on the unseen.

In direct contradiction to my reactions of hardship in years past, it remained evident that I did not place all my eggs in the basket of the complete miraculous healing of Ethan. All my eggs were placed in the basket of the goodness of God, His saving grace, and His glorious love for the world. This, in and of itself, proved to be the biggest miracle considering my jaded past.

Because of the powerful and profoundly transforming time surrounding the week of Ethan's death, there was nothing my soul cried out for more than to continue to experience this heaven on earth in the days, months, and years to follow. Given no choice other than to dive into a life now lived without Ethan, a life now lived without being called, "Mommy," my soul craved to continue to hear the voice of God. I was desperate to keep feeling the peace and the joy and the love I had been encountering so deeply.

It was when God met me in the places of deep and utter

sadness and the endless flow of tears that I heard Him speak. I felt His presence. I experienced His love lavished over me in a way I never had before.

About a month into enduring the heaviness of grieving Ethan, God was so gracious to give me such a beautiful vision in my mind of His love. The picture was of two big, yet gentle hands, palms facing up. In those hands, they were holding my heart, my actual bloody, gushing, broken, crushed, and barely beating heart. (I'm sorry for the gory detail here, but this image is so beautiful.) My heart had shattered and crushed into a gazillion pieces just dripping to the ground, sloppy and ugly and disgusting and pitiful.

It's almost as though as I saw the fragments of my heart seeping between the Father's fingers, His very own tears seeped through along with them.

God not only grieved alongside me, but He made promises that I held fast to and have seen come into fruition to this day. He makes promises, and He is faithful to fulfill them when we believe and move towards them. God promised that He would pick up every tiny little fragment of my heart, all the slop and mess on the ground, and piece it back together. He promised to make it more beautiful and stronger than it ever was before if I simply allowed God to bathe me in that love, trusting and pursuing Him.

He promised to turn this curse into blessing. He promised to make beauty from ashes. He promised to make me a Mommy again.

For evil comes to kill, steal, and destroy, but God comes to bring life and life more abundantly. God comes to bring justice and to payback what has been stolen. These are promises found in his Word that He makes to us when we choose to believe them and walk towards them.

How I deeply burned to be a mother again. As much as the loss of Ethan ripped me open, losing the title of "Mommy" was as significant of a hit. I had already waited so long for Ethan. And I was desperate for a baby sooner than Sam was ready for another one.

My soul ached in every moment to fill my arms again with a baby to love and care for. I spent hours and hours in prayer for the promise of Zoey. I knew beyond a shadow of a doubt *she* would arrive, even months before *she* was conceived, and what a gift *she* was. What a gift *she* is.

Zoey, in Greek meaning eternal life, was God's promise to us because out of death He promises us life. As Ethan has been given the gift of eternal life in heaven, we have been given a gift of life here on earth… Zoey, God's response and promise to bring heaven down along with Him. One of heaven's gift to us lived out on earth.

As I have fallen into a deeper pursuit of His love, His faithfulness stands. His love has never failed me. I see so much clearer now, and I have such a greater comprehension of that verse from 2 Corinthians that I reread so many times in the early days. I can see with a lens and perspective that my troubles now pale in comparison to the blessings He pours over me. I can see the promise of what is waiting for me in the life to come. I haven't grieved as the world grieves because I can now see the eternal. The world that we see with our eyes, it fades, it withers, it dies. But the world we cannot see lasts forever.

The unseen is where the power lies. The unseen is where I choose to steady my gaze.

Even though I am highly susceptible to anxiety and depression, I look back and can attest to the fact that during those three to six months following Ethan's death I was the most all-together healthy I have ever been in my entire life—emotionally, physically, mentally, and spiritually. How does one explain the reasoning behind this other than to say:

God.

His Love.

Jesus.

Yes, there have been seasons of dryness and failure and discouragement and falling back into old patterns of anxiety over the past five years, but it has all been a matter of brushing myself off, humbly realigning my heart with His, and moving forward into a new day. And with every new roadblock and glitch and shaking, as I utilize these principles and live them out in my heart on a daily basis, even through my grave weakness, I am an overcomer because the grace imparted by God moves me forward into a greater and greater strength. My eyes may see havoc surround me, but my spirit sees God's glory empower me.

It has gotten to the point where presently I stand in awe of the supernatural, His unexplainable working in my life, on a daily basis. There is no denying His presence. We have witnessed miracles and blessings that have blown our minds. Dreams have come true.

I believe that this is only the tip of the iceberg of what God wants to do. I can see His light shining all around me. It took me a while to learn, but it wasn't until I chose to take my vision off of myself and my problems and what I see around me that my perspective began to change. When I started to place my focus on Jesus, God gave me a completely new set of lenses.

My perspective has changed. My life has changed. I can see. There is no turning back. I have no desire in seeing the surface anymore. I want and will continue to pursue the treasures buried deep in His love, the unseen, as long as I live.

I do not mean to make light of such tragedy or anyone's hardship and struggle for that matter. I understand there are situations out there that people are forced to endure that are much more harrowing and horrific than mine.

In addition, if it seems as though I am bragging about my life, I am merely boasting about the glory of God I've invited to flow through it.

I am no golden child. Anyone can experience what I have. There is nothing different that exists in me than the promise of what exists in anyone else. I do not have more strength. If anything, in and of myself, I am much weaker than you. I am no less of a sinner. Chances are, I have failed greater than you.

I am far from perfect, far from capable in my own strength. It's all because of Him. His love. His Truth that has set me free. His Truth that allows me to see.

Go Deeper:

1. Reflect on 2 Corinthians 4:17-18 as written in the beginning of the chapter. What do these verses mean to you?

2. What patterns of fear exist in your life that prevent you from seeing through clear lenses?

3. What circumstance, past or present, do you feel you may be looking at through warped lenses? How does a belief in an eternal, loving, and perfect Father change your perspective on how you see that present circumstance and its outcome?

My Prayer:

God, it is hard to see my problems as small. So, help me to embrace the Truth that out of all the expanse of eternity, the blessings that await are far greater than any trial I go through in this day. I acknowledge that I see through warped lenses, to whatever degree of distortion that looks like. God, remove any fear and any deceptive thoughts or beliefs I hold that are preventing me from seeing the truth of the unseen. Instead, help me to engage and put into practice thought patterns that align with your Word. I pray that you give me a new set of lenses so that I am able to see your love and the world around me in the light of your Truth.

God's Promises:

Fix your thoughts on what is true, and honorable, and right, and pure, and lovely, and admirable. Think about things that are excellent and worthy of praise. Keep putting into practice all you learned and received from me—everything you heard from me and saw me doing. Then the God of peace will be with you.

Phil 4:8-9

Don't be misled—you cannot mock the justice of God. You will always harvest what you plant. Those who live only to satisfy their own sinful nature will harvest decay and death from that sinful nature. But those who live to please the Spirit will harvest everlasting life from the Spirit.

Galatians 6:7-8

Yet what we suffer now is nothing compared to the glory he will reveal to us later.

Romans 8:18

Now we see things imperfectly, like puzzling reflections in a mirror, but then we will see everything with perfect clarity. All that I know now is partial and incomplete, but then I will know everything completely, just as God now knows me completely.

1 Corinthians 13:12

So be truly glad. There is wonderful joy ahead, even though you must endure many trials for a little while. These trials will show that your faith is genuine. It is being tested as fire tests and purifies gold—though your faith is far more precious than mere gold. So when your faith remains strong through many trials, it will bring you much praise and glory and honor on the day when Jesus Christ is revealed to the whole world.

1 Peter 1:6

To all who mourn in Israel, he will give a crown of beauty for ashes, a joyous blessing instead of mourning, festive praise instead of despair. In their righteousness, they will be like great oaks that the Lord has planted for his own glory.

Isaiah 61:3

"No eye has seen, no ear has heard, and no mind has imagined what God has prepared for those who love him."

1 Corinthians 2:9

MY EYES MAY SEE
HAVOC SURROUND ME, BUT
MY SPIRIT SEES GOD'S
GLORY EMPOWER ME.

#LESSONSFROMAROCKSTAR

[twenty-two]

SURRENDER

Is there anyone out there who throws a party when they enter into a decision to surrender to something? Surrender for me, and I would undoubtedly believe for any sane person, is a word that our souls hear with a negative ring. It's a word that relays a feeling of losing control, incapability, giving up, defeat, and weakness, to name a few.

Does it make it any more reassuring for you to know that what God requires from us is a fully surrendered heart?

{Cringe} *Yikes!*

Whenever I sensed God wanted me to surrender in some capacity in the past, I would wince at the thought of the uncomfortable dreaded sacrifice I'd have to make. It seriously was like pulling teeth. My understanding was such that God wanted to take from me for the sake of taking from me. I hesitated often to give my heart up to God in surrender because I didn't trust He was faithful.

I want control, thank you very much! I didn't have a trusted understanding of the sole reason He wanted me to surrender my heart to Him—to fill me with the power of His love in as much as I emptied of myself.

But can I tell you, the more I have learned to surrender my heart to God, the more He fills me with His power. The more of myself I give to Him—my heart, my mind, my will, my emotions, my tongue, my eyes, my feet, my hands, my fears, my pride, my sin, my weaknesses, my strengths, my plans, my goals, my desires, my finances and on and on, my LIFE... the more He penetrates me with His love!

The more I lay myself down before Him and before others out of pure love, humility, and faith, the more I am able to receive from Him and the more I am changed and set free.

This may be the first time you are reading a spiritual book depicting Jesus as God. Maybe you never considered how a relationship with Jesus is not only beneficial during the destructive hardships of your life, but His life-transforming power is crucial even during your every-day life. If you are intrigued about Jesus from reading this book and want to know more about beginning a relationship with him, it all begins with surrendering your heart. A willingness to let go and trust. For it was Jesus who, first, surrendered his life for yours.

It doesn't mean you need to make drastic behavioral changes to "qualify" before coming to Him. Jesus is the one who has already qualified you, despite your disqualification. After all, everyone falls short of the glory of God and is in need of salvation. But you already have access to Him right here and right now through faith, by His grace, believing that He died for your sins and for the sins of the entire world. No matter the plunder and wreckage of your past and the turbulence of your today, He is waiting for your admission of brokenness and consent for Him to move you forward into the glory of a new day.

If this is something you want right now, here is an example of a prayer you can pray:

> *Jesus, I am broken. I have fallen short of your glory because I am human. In surrendering my heart to you, I acknowledge I am in need of your saving power. I believe that you chose to die for me because of your unfathomable love. I believe that the only one blameless, Jesus, took on the blame of the entire world and defeated death on the cross, all so that I would be given the gift of eternal life. I trust you to take my broken heart, and as I turn away from the darkness of my past, I choose to walk forward into the light of a new day. I pray you give me a new set of lenses so that I can be transformed by the Truth of your Word. In Jesus Name, Amen.*

On the other hand, you may be someone who has grown up going to Sunday School, reads the Bible regularly, serves or has served in church, or is connected to a church family. Allow this book to be a reminder that surrender is not just one occurrence during the moment of salvation, and then moments spread sporadically through the years in your walk with God. Sure, there are times when God asks us to specifically surrender in certain ways during appointed times, but we must remember most of all that surrender is a lifestyle. It is a continuous choice, a foundational attitude of a laid down life for Jesus.

Now that I have experienced God's faithfulness as I surrender to Him on deeper and deeper levels, I realize there is absolutely nothing to fear. The more I surrender, the more I encounter His glory and love that changes me and frees me from the inside out. It's still scary to take that first step out in faith and lose control, but ultimately, as I experience God's hand, I find surrender beautiful! To surrender is to experience more of the glorious power of His love!

I was able to make all the choices depicted in Part Two because I had a surrendered heart. When my heart is surrendered, I am able to put my hope in eternity. When my heart is surrendered, I can see God for who He truly is. When my heart is surrendered, a simple song is transformed into a weapon of the light and joy of worship. When my heart is surrendered, it unlocks the heavens to rain down its glory upon me.

God calls us to die to ourselves in order for us to gain everything we could ever imagine. We die to ourselves when we surrender our lives to Him. And He takes our heart and fills it with His goodness and Truth, bringing our desires in line with His. Ultimately, His desire is to make these God-aligned dreams come true in this life and the life to come.

This is what I know to be true:

I know at one point I surrendered my heart in the storm. I know I chose to believe that this is not the end. I know I asked God to heal my son. I know I chose to see God as a good Father. I know I chose to invite Him into the plunge with me. I know I chose to worship. And what I know beyond a shadow of a doubt is that, in doing so, I experienced heaven on earth. It wasn't enough to ask God to change my situation, but it became everything when I invited God into it. I continue to live in that place because of my surrendered heart and the glory and grace of God.

This whole journey has taught me a new way to live out my daily life. For me, it's a better way. It has proven to be my best way.

. . .

I don't know how dark your days are, and I don't pretend to have the answers for what you need to do for your circumstances to change. This is simply my story, outlining those choices I made during my darkest days—my dark night that turned into light, a curse turned into blessing, beauty made out of ashes.

Many have experienced the glory of God that I have experienced, so I don't believe I'm paving the way to anything new. In this book, I am not trying to challenge over 2,000 years of doctrine. I know nothing except my own experiences, which I have exposed through these vulnerable pages. I don't claim to be a qualified theologian. I am a mom, a wife, a daughter, and a human who has gone through what some would call the worst pain anyone could endure: burying their own child.

The only authority I can claim is to say, simply, that this is my story.

For so many years before, I angrily asked, "Why?" Now, the question that I like to answer rather than ask is: "Where was God?" My intention was to devote a section in Part Two answering this very question; however, I believe the answer has revealed itself over the course of this entire book. My hope is that as you grasp where God was during the loss of Ethan through my perspective, you will be able to answer that very question for yourself as you reflect on your own life. My prayer is that you would be able to see through new eyes, through a new set of lenses. Lenses of the Truth of God.

Ethan's death rocked me to the core in tribulation and grief. But through that pain, God's love rocked me to the core in a way that has forever changed me. God's love rocked me to the core in a way that I never want to look back.

With that, I carry a strong conviction that we are living in a day and age, amidst such oppressive darkness, where God wants to pour out His glory and healing miracles over the earth like He never has before. Just because Ethan passed on, it doesn't mean healing miracles can't be a part of your story. Pray and believe for supernatural miracles! Pray and believe for healing! Pray and believe for the glory of God to sweep over your situation as you surrender your heart!

I have a compelling sense that we are living in a time when heaven desires to come down to meet earth in a way the world has never known. Would you invite heaven to come down?

Eternal life, heaven on earth, is to be lived out right here, right now. Do you know it? Have you experienced it? Do you know peace, joy, love, and hope amidst your hardships? Do you experience the heavens opening upon your pain and suffering?

It is unmerited, completely accessible to anyone, the lowliest, most broken, and failure stricken person. I know this because that person... is me.

What if during the storms you face in life, God wants to inhabit that space with you? What if the miracles He wants to perform are such that you could not conceive? What if this is the age He desires to bring heaven down as we pray and declare, "Your kingdom come, your will be done, ON EARTH AS IT IS IN HEAVEN!" What if all we had to do is surrender our hearts, choose that this is not the end, believe in faith that He is good, acknowledge there are forces against God lying to us day in and day out, and invite Him to plunge into the depths with us in complete humility and surrender and thanksgiving?

What if God desires to blow your mind in the coming day and make your wildest dreams come true? Would you allow Him to rock you to your core in His love?

"Now to Him who is able to do exceedingly abundantly above all that we ask or think, according to the power that works in us, to Him be glory in the church by Christ Jesus to all generations, forever and ever. Amen." (Eph. 3:20)

HE rocked our lives. HE rocked our hearts. We will never be the same.

ABOUT THE AUTHOR

Kristen Lopez is a stay-at-home mom who has spent countless days changing dirty diapers and sifting through never-ending piles of laundry. She is an overcomer of child loss who has a passion for inspiring people to unlock the treasure within them to follow their God-given dreams, discovering they are fearlessly loved by their Creator. Born and raised in New Jersey, she currently resides there with her husband, Sam, of fourteen years and their three-year-old daughter, Zoey. Besides living out her passion serving on worship teams in churches throughout the years, Kristen loves spending quality time with friends and family and a good off-the-beaten-path travelling adventure somewhere around the world. It only took fifteen years, but she is finally the Disney fanatic Sam always dreamed she would become.